DOWN TO EARTH

WHY WE'RE REALLY HERE AND WHY IT MATTERS

DR. DAVID MCDONALD

Visit Dr. David McDonald's website at www.shadowinggod.com
Visit Samizdat Creative's website at www.samizdatcreative.com

ISBN-10: 0615335934
ISBN-13: 978-0-615-33593-3

Published in association with Westwinds Community Church, 1000 Robinson Road, Jackson, MI 49203
Published by Samizdat Creative, 5441 South Knox Court, Littleton, CO 80123.
All Scriptures used in this Atlas are taken from the NIV translation unless otherwise indicated.

This book was written primarily for the people of Westwinds Community Church in Jackson, Michigan. It is part of a series of similar books called "Teaching Atlases," which supplement David's sermons during the weekend worship services. They are part study-guide, part reminder, part artifact.

Additional Atlases can be obtained through the office of Westwinds Community Church on a host of other topics.

David is also available for guest teaching and lecturing and can be booked through his personal assistant, Norma Racey.

The set-up costs of each Atlas are privately donated by a Westwinds' parishioner, thus enabling extensive self-publishing at a reasonable cost. The proceeds from each Atlas are designated by the donor for a specific project—such as installing wells in developing countries, providing artistic and educational scholarships for children, or financially supporting pastors and missionaries around the world.

If you would like to donate to the Atlas project, please contact info@westwinds.org

DEDICATION

I just want to thank Westwinds for the opportunity to sponsor an Atlas for this series. I would also like to thank Janine McGill for all her hard work and time spent on getting donors. Janine has been very supportive through the entire process. I think this is a very special and worthwhile project.

I really don't have any words of wisdom to pass alone. My reason for sponsoring this Atlas is strictly personal. I wanted to expand my own personal walk with Jesus.

I felt I was getting into a rut. I would come to church each week, do my volunteer work as usual. I would attend what I felt was the mandatory meetings for an owner. It was getting quiet predictable. I do really love doing all of those things but nothing felt spontaneous any more. So last year I decided to change all that. I decided to do three things for the church I have never done before. I choose a staff member to do something nice for. It didn't have to be something fancy, it's the thought that counts and I wanted to let them know how much I appreciated their hard work.

I choose a youth to do something nice for. Again it could be mentor someone, words of wisdom, advise on a problem, help with the expense of a field trip or just take the young people a snack on Sunday night.

My third thing was to sponsor an Atlas for a series. I really like helping charity and giving when I can. To me there is nothing better. I liked it so much I'm doing that one again in 2010.

I have to wonder what could happen at Westwinds and in our community if all of us tried to get out of that rut and do just one thing for someone on our staff, a charity or something for the youth program. The possibilities are endless.

Thank You,

(the sponsor has asked to remain anonymous...they did say this was their personal journey with Jesus)

THE INCARNATION MEANS...

WE'RE CLEANSED BY THE ONE WHO BECAME SIN

WE SERVE BECAUSE OF THE ONE WHO DESCENDED

WE GO WITH THE ONE WHO CAME

WE SUFFER WITH THE ONE WHO DIED

WE WORSHIP THE ONE WHO SAVES

TABLE OF CONTENTS

INTRODUCTION

I've been trying to convince my son that God is not useless.

The other day we were having a rare family playtime. Jacob, my son, was pretending to be Superman; Carmel, my wife, was Wonder Woman; I was Wolverine (albeit in hibernation); and Papa, my father, said he wanted to be God.

To which my son replied that that would be no fun, since being God would require my dad to sit at the top of the stairs and do nothing.

Up there, doing nothing.

That sounds like a pretty accurate understanding of how our culture thinks of God – like a celestial referee who never calls anything, or a contractor (most likely escaped from Hell) who never bothers to visit his work site.

> God seems to have left the receiver off the hook.
> **Arthur Koestler, British author**
>
> It is left only to God and to the angels to be lookers on.
> **Francis Bacon, philosopher and scientist**

When we first heard Jake make that dismissive claim, our entire family (including him) laughed out loud. It's great when kids put their thoughts into simple, clear sound bytes like that.

But it's also a reason to sit down and have a chat.

The truth is that God is the exact opposite of a distant observer. He is most certainly not a clockmaker, creating the world and then resting on his holy laurels while the seconds tick by to Armageddon.

God is involved.

And I'm not talking about miracles
　　　(either verified or supposed)
　　or natural disasters
　　　　(disguised express tickets to either paradise or purgatory for saints and sinners, depending on their relative righteousness),
　　or even material blessings
　　　　(given to the good as a reward and the wicked as an indictment).

I'm talking about the central truth of Christian spirituality.

I'm talking about the Incarnation—about God becoming human and living among us.

God is so committed to this world and us who live in it, that He descended from His supposed throne of indifference and came here to see what things looked like from the ground up.
　　He was deeply invested in our daily affairs—
　　　　the humdrum and ho-hum of working,
　　　　　eating,
　　　　　laughing,
　　　　　sleeping,
　　　　　talking,
　　　　　playing,
　　　　　loving and all the rest –
　　　choosing to validate and authenticate every minute detail
　　　　of our clumsy, fumbling adventure
　　　　　on this blue marble planet.

The Incarnation (latin, by the way, for in [in] flesh [carno]) shows us that God is a committed parent playing with His children on the rug, even when they decide to kill Him off.

This book is about the Incarnation...and I'm writing it because I'm afraid that my son is not the only one who's forgotten just how involved God was then and remains now in the lives of His children.

> I'm writing to educate
>> because I am saddened at just how few Christians I speak to know why the Incarnation is more than just a theological abstraction; and
>
> I'm writing to inspire,
>> because knowing who God really is
>>> and how He really works
>>> really does change our perception
>>> of why we're really here
>>>> and what really matters.

Our beliefs work like the control room for our lives: What we believe most deeply most fully controls how we live.

Based on the way we live, I'm hard-pressed to see much similarity between Western Christians and Jesus Christ. That's not to say that Western Christians are horrible, lousy, miserably shallow human train wrecks...just that—somewhere, somehow—we've forgotten just who Jesus was and what he came to show us.

He came to show us how to live, how to be human.

And here are the five colossal truths in which we engage through his Incarnation:

- ☐ Salvation – we're cleansed by the One who became sin
  > Dark and rotten in our sinfulness, it is only because of Jesus Christ's sacrificial death on the cross that we have access to God.

- ☐ Kenosis – we serve because of the One who descended
  > Jesus divested himself of his divine privileges, so we too must let go of the privileges we have in this world and wholly devote ourselves to serving God and other people.

☐ Mission – we go with the One who came
> Jesus came to save and heal the world, restoring a fallen creation to a loving Creator. Because of our allegiance to Jesus, our purpose in this life is to heal the world.

☐ Solidarity – we suffer with the One who died
> When we suffer, we take comfort from knowing Jesus also suffered. When others suffer, we too come alongside them to bear witness and give comfort.

☐ Confession – we worship the One who saves
> Christianity is about Jesus Christ—the One above whom there is no other, God-made-flesh, eternal, and cosmic. We worship him because he saved us from sin, corruption, and judgment.

These towering truths are not merely technicalities or data, and I caution you not to file them under "things-I-should-probably-memorize-but-don't-really-care-about." Each of these truths will lead to remarkable personal transformation if you live by them.

You will be different once you encounter Christ.

Which is, after all, the whole point of the Incarnation to begin with.

Read on.
Rock on.

D.

CHALCEDONIAN CREED

(written 451 AD, for the purpose of clarifying Jesus' Incarnation)

We, then, following the holy Fathers,
    all with one consent,
    teach people to confess
        one and the same Son,
        our Lord Jesus Christ,
            the same perfect in Godhead
            and also perfect in manhood;

truly God and truly man, of a reasonable [rational] soul and body;

consubstantial [co-essential] with the Father
    according to the Godhead, and
consubstantial with us
    according to the Manhood;

in all things like unto us, without sin;

begotten before all ages of the Father according to the Godhead,
    and in these latter days,
    for us and for our salvation,
born of the Virgin Mary, the Mother of God,
        according to the Manhood;

one and the same Christ,
    Son,
    Lord,
    only begotten,
to be acknowledged in two natures,
    inconfusedly,
    unchangeably,
    indivisibly,
    inseparably;

the distinction of natures being by no means taken away by the union,
but rather the property of each nature being preserved,
and concurring in one Person
and one Subsistence,
not parted or divided into two persons,
but one and the same Son,
and only begotten,
God the Word,
the Lord Jesus Christ;

as the prophets from the beginning have declared concerning Him,
and the Lord Jesus Christ Himself has taught us,
and the Creed of the holy Fathers
has handed down to us.

down to earth

PART ONE: SALVATION

WE'RE CLEANSED BY THE ONE WHO BECAME SIN

*Jesus took our sin and shame. He took care of them forever on the Cross.
Because of the Incarnation we are saved.*

In the beginning was the Word,
     and the Word was with God,
     and the Word was God.

He was in the beginning with God.

All things were made through Him,
     and without Him nothing was made that was made.

In Him was life,
     and the life was the light of men.
       And the light shines in the darkness,
         and the darkness did not comprehend it.

There was a man sent from God, whose name was John. This man came for a witness, to bear witness of the Light, that all through him might believe. He was not that Light, but was sent to bear witness of that Light. That was the true Light which gives light to every man coming into the world.

He was in the world,
     and the world was made through Him,
     and the world did not know Him.

He came to His own,
     and His own did not receive Him.

     But as many as received Him,
       to them He gave the right to become children of God,
       to those who believe in His name:
         who were born, not of blood,
         nor of the will of the flesh,
         nor of the will of man,
           but of God.

And the Word became flesh and dwelt among us,
     and we beheld His glory,
     the glory as of the only begotten of the Father,
       full of grace and truth.

John 1.1-14 NKJV

'A cold coming we had of it,
Just the worst time of the year
For the journey, and such a long journey:
The ways deep and the weather sharp,
The very dead of winter.'
And the camels galled, sore-footed, refractory,
Lying down in the melting snow.
There were times we regretted
The summer palaces on slopes, the terraces,
And the silken girls bringing sherbet.
Then the camel men cursing and grumbling
And running away, and wanting their liquor and women,
And the night-fires going out, and the lack of shelters,
And the cities hostile and the towns unfriendly
And the villages dirty and charging high prices:
A hard time we had of it.
At the end we preferred to travel all night,
Sleeping in snatches,
With the voices singing in our ears, saying
That this was all folly.

      Then at dawn we came down to a temperate valley,
      Wet, below the snow line, smelling of vegetation;
      With a running stream and a water-mill beating the darkness,
      And three trees on the low sky,
      And an old white horse galloped away in the meadow.
      Then we came to a tavern with vine-leaves over the lintel,
      Six hands at an open door dicing for pieces of silver,
      And feet kicking the empty wine-skins,
      But there was no information, and so we continued
      And arrived at evening, not a moment too soon
      Finding the place; it was (you may say) satisfactory

All this was a long time ago, I remember,
And I would do it again, but set down
This set down
This: were we led all that way for
Birth or Death? There was a Birth, certainly,
We had evidence and no doubt. I had seen birth and death,
But had thought they were different; this Birth was
Hard and bitter agony for us, like Death, our death,
We returned to our places, these Kingdoms,
But no longer at ease here, in the old dispensation,
With an alien people clutching their gods.
I should be glad of another death.

The Journey of the Magi
T.S. Eliot

AVATAR

In the beginning was the Word,
    and the Word was with God,
    and the Word was God.

He was in the beginning with God.

All things were made through Him,
    and without Him nothing was made that was made.

In Him was life,
    and the life was the light of men.
        And the light shines in the darkness,
            and the darkness did not comprehend it.

There was a man sent from God, whose name was John. This man came for a witness, to bear witness of the Light, that all through him might believe. He was not that Light, but was sent to bear witness of that Light. That was the true Light which gives light to every man coming into the world.

He was in the world,
    and the world was made through Him,
    and the world did not know Him.

He came to His own,

and His own did not receive Him.
But as many as received Him,
> to them He gave the right to become children of God,
> to those who believe in His name:
>> who were born, not of blood,
>> nor of the will of the flesh,
>> nor of the will of man,
>>> but of God.

And the Word became flesh and dwelt among us,
> and we beheld His glory,
> the glory as of the only begotten of the Father,
>> full of grace and truth.

John 1.1-14 NKJV

It seems incarnations are all the rage these days. Both the Bruce Willis flop *Surrogate* and the James Cameron blockbuster *Avatar* are about humans with flesh-and-blood incarnations.

Both Playstation Home and Second Life are communities of computer-controlled incarnations (called an "avatar") through whom users live vicariously.

Both Rastafarianism and Kabbalah have contemporary incarnations of their deities (Haile Selassie for the former and pretty much everyone else for the latter).

But why is this idea so popular? And why now? Where did the idea of an incarnation come from? And who can tell what's worthwhile and what's whacky?

For starters, it may be important to acknowledge that many of our filmmakers and novelists grew up in a Western civilization dominated by Christian themes and values. Whether or not these artists consider themselves Christians is almost irrelevant—the cultural environment shapes our thoughts and the stories we draw from, regardless of whether we want it to or not.

It's part of our cultural heritage.

Which is to say, that our interest in Incarnation comes *from* somewhere: It comes from the ground water of the Christian story.

In this story, the Incarnation is the act of grace whereby Christ merged his Divine nature with a human one.

In him there are two natures—
human and divine—
each retaining its own properties,
and united in a single person.

Christ is both God and man.

This doctrine is known as the Hypostatic Union
(from *homoousia* meaning "from the same stuff")
and is closely related to the doctrine of the Trinity—
which is the idea that God exists in one substance
but three Persons (Father, Son, and Holy Spirit).

The Hypostatic Union was formally adopted by the Church at the Council of Chalcedon in 451 A.D. in order to bring clarity to this part of the Scriptures.

And the Scriptures did—and still do—need clarification. For example, the central text dealing with the Incarnation is the opening hymn of the gospel of John.

It can be confusing for the non-theologian/historian/philosopher to understand without help.

Which is to say that no one understands it, at first.

In the hymn, John gives us some important information about Christ.
First off, he identifies Jesus Christ as the Word—
the same Word, in fact,
that was Present in creation (Genesis 1.1-2)
which also happens to be the same Word
that was Personified in Proverbs 8 as Wisdom.

According to the Proverbs,
no one in the world
wanted to make room for Wisdom;
but, according to John, Wisdom—the Word—
has now found a home among the
followers of Jesus Christ.

Furthermore, this Word has now become flesh. Jesus is this Word.
More to the point, since this Word is the Creator made human,
we get to catch a glimpse into the Creator's mission and
method:

God became flesh in order to identify with us,
>
> So He could save us,
>
> And with us, heal the world.

The Creat(or)
> became the Creat(ed)
> in order to give new life to Creat(ion).

Scott McKnight

For He became man that we might become divine;
> and He revealed Himself through a body
> that we might receive an idea of the invisible Father;
> and He endured insults from men
>> that we might inherit incorruption

St. Athanasius

This is far more detail than most of us think we need about Jesus, but it's important. In the end you'll have a much stronger understanding of what it means to be connected to your Creator and (perhaps more importantly) why that connection matters. In fact, I even notice a difference in my son since we've began having our little chats about the Incarnation (and, yes, I know it's a little crazy to force your six-year-old into deep theological discussion). Though he can't articulate it well, Jacob already has a good understanding of these two main ideas:

Christ knows what we're going through,
> Christ can help us get through it.

As a result, Jake is quick to turn to God in prayer for help when he gets hurt, or peace when he gets angry.

He's actually better at that than I am.

And that's the point, isn't it? The real reason we're investigating this issue isn't so that we can brag about our keen understanding of theology, but so our lives will be different.

Because we need help,
> and we need peace,
>> and we need Jesus.

QUESTIONS FOR FURTHER REFLECTION

1. There is quite a bit of doctrine in this chapter, which many people find boring. Knowing that this doctrine is critical to your Christian experience, how might you ensure you best understand it? Can you compare it to anything in order to help it make better sense? Can you think of anyone who might be able to explain it to you more clearly?

2. Had you ever connected the idea of computer avatars with the Incarnation of Jesus? In what ways do these comparisons hold? In what ways do they differ? Can you think of other comparisons that might be more accurate?

3. In your own words, try and describe the "Hypostatic Union." What does it mean to you that Christ was both God and man?

DISNEY AND THE DIVINE

Only now that I have a daughter do I have any real awareness of Disney films.

Seriously, *Finding Nemo,*
      Pocahontas,
      The Lion King,
      Cinderella,
      Beauty and the Beast,
          and *Aladdin* are all mainstays at the McDonald household
          because my beautiful banAnna loves those Disney princesses.

Her favorite?

Hands down – *The Little Mermaid.*

Like any good Dad I indulge my daughter by sitting next to her on the couch while this movie plays. But, all beliefs about my infallible holiness to the contrary, I also tend to nap through it.

On one particularly caffeinated day, however, I stayed awake through The Little Mermaid and discovered something quite profound.

Theology.

Like many Disney films, *The Little Mermaid* has a functional Christology at the heart of the narrative.

Or—to say it like a human being instead of a dictionary—a lot of the heroes in Disney films give up their lives in order to save the people they love, just like Jesus Christ gave up his life in order to save us.

In this film King Triton, Ariel's (the titular character's) father, trades his life for hers after she fails to satisfy the terms of her agreement with the Sea Witch Ursula. This transaction leaves King Triton at the bottom of the ocean powerless and formless, a soul without a body, stuck in an existential oceanic penal colony.

I don't want to risk interpreting any more of the film in light of Christian theology than I have to, but suffice to say King Triton's sacrifice on behalf of his daughter is a sacrifice like that of Jesus.

It is that sacrifice—Jesus' sacrifice—that concerns us here in this chapter. But, to better contextualize what he did and why he had to, let's rewind the story back to the beginning.

In the beginning, God creates a perfect world—where everyone and everything enjoys unbroken harmony (Genesis 1-2). Humanity is given a status like that of a viceroy or regent, made responsible for the well-being of creation on behalf of the ultimate Creator, God (Genesis 2.15-20).

Into this idyllic setting something ugly comes, and through the first act of disobedience to God, sin enters the world. Adam and Eve, the first couple and our spiritual parents, disobey the one edict God had given them (Genesis 3.1-7). Consequently, a gap opens up between them and their God (Genesis 3.13-19).

This sin-gap is a substantial problem. A perfectly holy God cannot stand to be in the presence of imperfection (2 Peter 2.4-10). Sin is, at least, imperfection; though, to be fair, it's much more like contamination. God sets about restoring His broken relationship with His Creation through a series of Covenants:

> Through **Abraham** (Genesis 15), God chooses a holy people and plans to heal the world through their cooperation with Him. Sadly, they pretty much decline to cooperate, and the world is not healed nor are the people completely reunited with their Creator.

> Through **Moses** (Exodus 20), God chooses a collection of laws and rituals that will guide the people to live well and experience His unity once more. Again, this interests the people less than serving their own interests and essentially telling God to take a hike.

Through King **David** (2 Samuel 7), God chooses to establish His dominion and authority in Israel to show the world what godly power and care looks like in a model of the restoration of Eden. Once more, however, the people—particularly the kings who succeed King David—show little interest in God's plan to heal the world. They'd rather control it themselves.

Through the **Prophets** (Isaiah 1, Ezekiel 2, Jeremiah 3), God chooses to speak about Justice and Mercy and a Return to Righteousness. Yet, again, the people only give nominal attention to these concerns and focus their activities on getting along with the dominant forces of economy, politics, and culture in hopes of self-preservation.

And so God collects the broken strands of humanity and of their failed covenants with Him, and crafts a New Covenant (first mentioned in Jeremiah 31.31-34), a new plan for restoring a fallen creation back to its original splendor.

This New Covenant collects a Holy **People** (1 Peter 2.9) much like the Covenant with Abraham was supposed to, only now these people are not delineated by ethnicity but by allegiance to God.

This New Covenant has a new set of **laws** written on the human heart, not on stone tablets, and this new law is summed up in Loving God and Loving others (Matthew 22.34-40).

This New Covenant has a Kingdom **authority** to it, but the new Kingdom works like a franchise with each Person carrying the Kingdom inside of them (Luke 17.21).

This New Covenant **values** Justice and Mercy and Righteousness, but they aren't just words or ideals. They are lived out in a community of believers who have aligned themselves with God and His People, empowered and sent forth by His Holy Spirit (Acts 2.42-47).

The New Covenant is this:

Jesus Christ,
both fully God and fully man,
came to live in this world
for the sole purpose of repairing creation
and reconciling man to God (John 3.16-17).
He lived as we should be living (1 Corinthians 11.1).

Though guiltless of any crime (2 Corinthians 5.21),
    Jesus was executed on the Cross of Calvary
    for the crimes of all humanity (1 Peter 3.18)
        by representatives of political, religious, and spiritual
        corruption.

He was a scapegoat (Hebrews 9-10).

His death was a sacrifice.

    His death paid off any spiritual debt
        the rest of the world owed to God
            for our imperfection,
            our corruption,
            our rebellion,
            our self-interest,
                and our sin (John 1.29).

His blood was like spiritual liquid paper,
    blotting out all our misdeeds
        on the records of eternity.

He paid a terrible price that,
    for all intents and purposes,
        was a price we ourselves should have paid
            for the sins we recklessly
                and franticly
            commit in our efforts
                to be our own People,
                write our own laws,
                build our own little
                    kingdoms,
                and justify our own
                    indulgences.

Now, just as sin came into the world
        through the disobedience of one man,
            Adam,
    it was depleted by the sacrifice of one man,
            Jesus Christ,
        whose perfection exposed the weakness
            and emptiness of sin (Romans 5.12).
Jesus came into new life,
    having been resurrected from death

and having exposed the limitation of sin's power
to separate us from the life God intended us
to have (1 Corinthians 15.20-28).

We participate in this New Covenant,
God's absolute plan for healing the world
and restoring unity between Creation and Creator,
through repenting our old way of living
and placing our hope in Jesus Christ,
Savior of the world (Mark 1.15).

That, I know, was a fair amount of information to absorb...maybe more than you were thinking this book would contain. But I am convinced now more than ever before in my short life that those details matter.

You have to understand just how comprehensive,
how involved,
how complicated,
and how powerful the death of Jesus really was
so you can begin to understand how comprehensive,
how involved,
how liberating,
and how powerful your new life
in Christ Jesus can be.

So my friend, Ryan (not his real name), grows up in church hearing about the grace of God and the sacrifice of Jesus his whole life but lives like a complete idiot because he only knows one side of the coin. All he knows is that God forgives us when we sin, but Ryan has no concept of the lengths to which God has gone to forgive that sin. Ryan has no clue that God cannot merely disregard our sins, but actually has to deal with them. Ryan has no concept of how painful it is for God to see him incur such a sin-debt, and so he lives with a disregard for God's grace.

For Ryan, asking for forgiveness of God Almighty is like remembering to say thank you on Christmas. It's required, but just barely, and it never interferes with whether or not he gets presents.

As a result, Ryan's life is robbed of meaning. He takes no comfort in God's grace because it's a formula. He still feels soiled, even after asking for forgiveness, because he thinks he's been given a hand-me-down pair of shoes instead of the single greatest gift in the universe.

Ryan's cheap understanding of grace doesn't just offend God, it hurts Ryan. It steals the only real chance he's got to feel clean.

Eventually, Ryan figures some stuff out. He dives into Scripture. He gets a mentor. He's held accountable for his indulgence.

Lo and behold! Ryan starts to understand just how precious a gift Jesus' atoning death really is.

> Because Ryan knows his sins have been crucified with Christ, he's able to enjoy their absence.

> Because he knows that Christ had to be crucified to get rid of those sins, he's reluctant to commit any more, especially not through his carelessness or lack of attention.

> Because he knows that Christ willingly died not just to get rid of sin, but more importantly to give Ryan new life, he's happier...more able to enjoy life...more free from guilt, from distraction, from temptation, from the stain of his mistakes.

Ryan's is a story I've seen retold in the lives of countless Christians who finally come to understand the tremendous cost Jesus Christ has paid for our sinless standing before a Holy God.

Once you begin to understand what your sin costs, and what it cost Christ, you begin to understand your true wealth and wealth in the world as someone free and clean.

QUESTIONS FOR FURTHER REFLECTION

1. What would you do if someone told you everything in this chapter was a lie and that none of it was actually in the Bible? What would you do if someone told you that none of the Scripture verses used in this chapter actually supported the things they are meant to support? Obviously, you'd look them up and check for yourself. Allow us to suggest you do that now. What impact do these Scriptures have on you when you read them altogether? How do they change your perceptions of Jesus and his death on the cross?

2. Besides the character of King Triton in The Little Mermaid, can you think of any other "Christ-figures" in film or television? In what ways are these portrayals helpful to your spiritual journey? In what ways might they be misleading?

3. Of the four covenants referenced in this chapter from the First Testament (Abraham, Moses, David, the Prophets), which is the most interesting to you? Why? Can you think of a contemporary parallel to these covenants (i.e. can you think of any religious groups that are centered on a certain ethnic group, or certain laws, or a certain leader, or a certain value system)? What would you tell these people about Jesus?

SIN SUICIDE

For he hath made him to be sin for us, who knew no sin; that we might be made the righteousness of God in him.
2 Corinthians 5:21

I think almost everyone I know feels—or has often felt—worthless. We get this distinct impression, at times, like we don't matter or we're not good enough or that the world would be better off without our pervasive stupidity.

Immature Christians—as well as a host of well-wishers, New Agers, and soccer moms—try to convince us in those moments that we are not worthless. That we are, in fact, worthy of every good thing the universe should send our way.

They're not right.

Angry Christians—those who love doctrine and dogma, theology and law— try to convince us that this worthlessness is God-given, a reminder that we are broken, fallen, foolish, and evil.

They're not right either.

If somehow we could combine the warm heart of the first group with the difficult truth of the second, we might approach something resembling the truth.

Because the truth is...
>you're not worthy of love, of grace, of forgiveness.

Truth is...
>we're not capable of consistent selflessness,
>>compassion,
>>brotherly love,
>>>and altruism.

Truth is...
>much of the guilt we feel, we've earned,
>>and deep down we know it.

>>So we either try to bury what we know to be true
>>>because it hurts,
>>or we let it consume us
>>>and become unable to experience
>>>>real joy,
>>>>real peace,
>>>>or real happiness in this lifetime.

This, by the way, is so far the single most depressing thing I've ever written.

But it gets better.

Though we are indeed fallen, broken, selfish creatures when left to our own devices, we were not meant to be that way. We can be different, not through our own efforts, but through a process of spiritual healing.

We can live differently, wholly, in peace and love, when we allow Christ to penetrate our sin and infect us with himself.

By cooperating with Christ, by allowing God to work through us, by inviting the Holy Spirit to change our hearts and edit our attitudes, we can become the people we all know we should be.

We can become like God—not gods ourselves, mind you—but like God. We can each become the kind of person that Jesus was...without, of course, ever being equal to him.

>We cannot totally break from the limits of our humanity. Yet Christ's death and resurrection inaugurate something new within our lives

that will ultimately unseat our former master, undo our bonds to our past ways of living and thinking, and unleash the full power of God's grace to heal and to transform.
Allister McGrath

Let's see if we can fill out this argument a little more:

Since we have all sinned (Romans 3.23)
> and our sins separate us from God (Isaiah 59.2)
> we rightly feel terrible
>> about being apart from our Creator,
>>> for whom we were designed for relationship, (Genesis 1.27-28; Jeremiah 1.5)
>> and for being the cause of that separation (1 John 1.8).

Additionally, God cannot disregard our sin.
> Our sin must be dealt with,
> and it incurs a penalty: death (Romans 6.23).

Again, this should cause us to feel pretty insecure,
> unworthy,
>> and anxious about our standing before God.

Fortunately for us, knowing that our efforts to live sinless lives without his help would be useless, God Himself came here to take our sin (1 John 4.10).

> In fact, He went to the extreme, sending Jesus Christ to actually become sin (2 Corinthians 5.21) in the all-time greatest ruse of meta-human history.

By becoming sin and going willfully to the Cross, Jesus basically killed sin itself (1 Peter 2.24; 3.18).

Sin is dead (Ephesians 2.1-5).
> The power of sin has been exhausted (Colossians 2.15).

But the story isn't over.

Sin may have been put to death with Christ on the cross,
> but Christ didn't stay dead.
>> Through his resurrection,
>>> Jesus makes new life available to all who believe in him (Romans 6.1-14). This new life available to those who love and follow Jesus is free from the power of sin, the guilt that rightly accompanies sin, and restores to every believer our intended position as children of God (Romans 8.14-17).

Let's see if we can bring this around to something resembling a point.

> Christ fixed our sin problem
>> by becoming sin
>>> and committing sin-suicide.

> Through his resurrection,
>> we get new life free from the power of the sin he killed.

> New life is the life we've always known we should have had...
>> free from guilt,
>> from shame,
>> from crushing doubt and painful absence,
>> from the bondage to our addictions
>>> and the enslavement of our base desires.

We get that.

We get to have our filth washed away, our painful memories scrubbed, and our decisions liberated from a lifetime of regret.

And though we have a responsibility to cooperate with God as He leads us in this new life, it is not our efforts to succeed that will ultimately make or break us. Our own individual power to defeat sin is still insufficient, and only when we realize that and allow God's sin-crushing power to work through us will we be able to experience the freedom, the joy, and the hope that comes in Christ Jesus.

> Everything I do to be a better person is as useless as doing CPR on a corpse. Because of my baptism into the one who is The Way, The Truth, The Life, I now have the privilege of living Jesus' resurrection

life in the world...I am collaborating with God's inbreaking Advent.
Len Sweet

Once we stop trying to conquer sin on our own—once we stop trying to get rid of that worthless, useless feeling without actually acknowledging that it is too big for us—then we can receive God's free gift of grace and begin living the life He always intended for us to enjoy.

QUESTIONS FOR FURTHER REFLECTION

1. Have you ever felt worthless? Useless? What did you do to try and countermand that feeling? How did you fight it? Were you successful?

2. This chapter started out with a heavy bit of bad news – that we're not, in and of ourselves worthy – and then began to share some of the good news. Did that, in fact, feel like good news? Has your perspective on God's grace changed at all by reading this chapter?

3. Briefly reflect on the quote from Len Sweet ("everything I do to be a better person is as useless as doing CPR on a corpse"). How accurate do you think that statement is?

THE RIDICULOUS SELF-IMPROVEMENT GENE

His divine power has given us everything we need for life and godliness through our knowledge of him who called us by his own glory and goodness. Through these he has given us his very great and precious promises, so that through them you may participate in the divine nature and escape the corruption in the world caused by evil desires.
2 Peter 1.3-4

Be transformed by the renewing of your mind.
Romans 12.2b

My wife, Carmel, has a condition we jokingly call "the ridiculous self-improvement gene", though it's a bit of a misnomer. She's not really that interested in "self-improvement." No—her commitment to being a changed person goes deeper than that.

It began through her relationship with a gal named Jen McPherson. Jen worked for Campus Crusade, a Christian organization that works in local colleges, and she was Carmel's spiritual mentor for several years. Jen was a terrific example of a godly woman, deeply committed to her faith in Jesus Christ and to a life of ongoing transformation.

Jen wanted to be the kind of person God created her to be, and she passed that desire on to my wife.

Consequently, both Jen and Carmel would spend hours studying the Bible, praying, chatting with other people who loved and followed Jesus about how to mature as Christians. That noble ambition—to become increasingly saturated by the Spirit of Jesus—has stayed with my wife ever since.

For example, when Carmel gets criticized, her first reaction is pretty much like everyone else's, I suppose, but it doesn't stop there. Carmel tries to sort out the hurtful bits of the criticism from the bits that may actually be true. She asks God to help her get over the bad bits and learn from the true bits.

And she keeps on changing.

I've had to learn how to do that from her. I confess a sort of puppy-dog optimism about life in general and my own pleasantness in particular. I tend to think that everything is great until it's not, and then when it's not great I tend to think it's an easy fix and—in what may be my one redeeming quality—I'll get to work right away fixing it.

But if it's not an easy fix, then I get mad. I get controlling. I get intense and domineering, all because it must be someone else's inability to change that is causing this problem to continue.

Right.

Those are the moments in which where Carmel has helped me to understand that I have to grow as a person.

She's helped me see that growth doesn't happen just through my own efforts, but by cooperating with the Holy Spirit who is making me new from the inside out.

Some of my experiences as a parent illustrate for me, and hopefully for you, how this cooperation with God works.

I like walking with my little kids. They're completely enamored with the outdoors, and its fun to see them react to every little bird and branch. Sometimes, though, when we come to a steep hill both of my kids feign paraplegia. They pretend they can't walk, or are too weak to get up the hill. Sometimes the hill really is too steep for them, and so I hold their hand. I do all the work to get them up the hill, but without carrying them. I still want them to walk because I want them to get stronger. I won't work unless they do, and as soon as they make any effort I do my part and help them up the hill.

You and I, too, have a responsibility to cooperate with God in our personal transformation, but it is still God who moves us forward. Spiritual transformation is not instantaneous, it is a lifelong process of inviting the Spirit to live in me and Christ to work through me—a lifelong journey of holding on to God and trusting Him for progress.

Did I mention that it's hard?

This, I suppose, is why many people who claim to be lovers and followers of Jesus seem to change so little over the years. For some, it may be that they're lazy, or that they don't want to change; but—and here comes my puppy-dog optimism again—for others it may simply be that change is hard.

> It's hard to stop gossiping about others.
>> It's hard to become more generous and less tight-fisted.
>> It's hard to follow the sexual norms in the Scriptures.
>> It's hard to divest yourself of your privilege and wealth.
>> It's hard to serve others.
> It's hard to control what you say, how you say it, and to whom.

It's hard.

In many ways, the Christian life is like owning a foreign-made car. I own such a car, a 1999 Land Rover. It's the kind of vehicle I've always wanted. It's cool. It's a man-mobile with great off-road capabilities, but it's also comfortable with a leather interior and twin sun roofs. It's also constantly in need of very expensive repairs. (Apparently, the British don't make cars to last any longer than their colonization of small, out of the way, countries.)

Anyway, in order to keep my Rover running, I've got to keep repairing it.

In order to keep your faith growing, you've got to keep asking God to repair you. You've got to constantly cooperate with the work of the Spirit to increasingly become the person God intended you to be.

You will always undergo spiritual repair and restoration.

That's what it means to be a disciple.

But—and I cannot stress this enough—this transformation is not something we achieve on our own. We have to make the effort, but the transformation only occurs as we allow the power of the Spirit to work in us.

In this way, spiritual development is like a kind of pregnancy. We feel the Spirit gestating in us. We look after the Spirit-in-us so that it grows up, and grows larger within us, working to be born. In the Eastern Orthodox church, they refer to this as *theotokos*.

It means God-bearing.

For many Christians, the reason the Virgin Mary is so important is because she models for us what every believer should be doing: we should all allow Christ to be born in us.

> He is born in Bethlehem in order that he may be born in us.
> **Meister Eckhart**

> The Incarnation is always happening.
> **St. Augustine**

> Christ is always waiting to be born, asking for room in our hearts.
> **Dorothy Day**

> Of what benefit would it be to me if Christ had been born a thousand times...if he were never born in me.
> **Martin Luther**

> The soul of a monk is a Bethlehem where Christ comes to be born.
> **Thomas Merton**

What I mean by that, indeed what has always been meant by that, is that we give permission to the Spirit to take root in our hearts,
> to affect our decision-making,
> to infect our opinions and diminish our judgment of others,
> to alter our thinking from the downtrodden,
>> hope-robbed thoughts of this world's nihilism
>> into the enthusiastic thoughts of God-possibilities.

The Spirit gestates in us, grows in us, takes shape in us, feeding our desire for cooperation with God, like a child in a womb.

There is a big difference between what we're talking about here—the participation in the divine nature, as Peter calls it in his second letter—and simply trying to imitate Jesus.

In fact, the imitation of Christ is quite misleading (full apologies to Thomas à Kempis). Trying to imitate his perfection often leaves us feeling like frustrated failures because we're not supposed to be copying Christ...we're supposed to be filled with Christ. The former is just behavior modification, the latter is Incarnation.

> Christ is born in us,
>> rejuvenating us,
>> working within us to bring life
>>> and light
>>> and healing
>>> and hope.

The difference between behavioral modification and Incarnation is like the difference between a mounted knight and a Centaur. A knight in shining armor may love his horse, may even depend on his horse during battle and trust it with his life, but in the end they're different creatures.

But not us. No! Through our acceptance of God's grace we are like Centaurs— human and horse together in one creature.

> We cannot be separated from Christ (Romans 8.35),
>> and it is his Spirit that lives in us,
>> animates us (1 Corinthians 15.44),
>>> and is constantly working inside of us for his glory.

This is our new identity as lovers and followers of Christ, and the process of transformation is the process in which we gradually actualize our Centaur-ness rather than our mounted-knight-ness.

It's one of the reasons I'm drawn to the distinction between human being and human becoming.

Always remember that we are works in progress, and that it's the work of the Spirit that actually progresses us.

QUESTIONS FOR FURTHER REFLECTION

1. Who do you know that has a "ridiculous self-improvement gene?" How does their example compare with that of Carmel and Jen in the story that opens this chapter? What can you learn from them, without falling into the trap of thinking that it is solely your effort that progresses you spiritually?

2. Look up 2 Peter 1.3-4. Read it carefully. What do you think Peter means by being "participants in the Divine Nature?" How can you apply that in real life? How can you keep that participation in mind throughout your week?

3. Reflect on the illustration of the foreign-made car. How important is it for us to be undergoing constant spiritual repair and restoration? Who do you have in your life that helps you understand when, and where, you need this kind of work to be done in your soul?

4. What do you think about this idea of *theotokos*, of Christ being born in you? In what ways is this different than thinking about the imitation of Christ? Did the example of the knight and the Centaur make this clearer for you? If so, how?

RUIN THE PARTY IN HEAVEN

Therefore, just as sin entered the world through one man, and death through sin, and in this way death came to all men, because all sinned — for before the law was given, sin was in the world. But sin is not taken into account when there is no law. Nevertheless, death reigned from the time of Adam to the time of Moses, even over those who did not sin by breaking a command, as did Adam, who was a pattern of the one to come.

But the gift is not like the trespass. For if the many died by the trespass of the one man, how much more did God's grace and the gift that came by the grace of the one man, Jesus Christ, overflow to the many! Again, the gift of God is not like the result of the one man's sin: The judgment followed one sin and brought condemnation, but the gift followed many trespasses and brought justification. For if, by the trespass of the one man, death reigned through that one man, how much more will those who receive God's abundant provision of grace and of the gift of righteousness reign in life through the one man, Jesus Christ.

Consequently, just as the result of one trespass was condemnation for all men, so also the result of one act of righteousness was justification that brings life for all men. For just as through the disobedience of the one man the many were made sinners, so also through the obedience of the one man the many will be made righteous.

The law was added so that the trespass might increase. But where sin

increased, grace increased all the more, so that, just as sin reigned in death, so also grace might reign through righteousness to bring eternal life through Jesus Christ our Lord.
Romans 5.12-21

Michael Vick, the current quarterback for the Philadelphia Eagles, has just been released from serving 18 months in prison. He was convicted of felony charges for running a dog-fighting ring.

One of the things I hear most about Vick is that he's *inhuman.*

That's a pretty devastating accusation if you think about it, one usually reserved for the likes of Nero, Goering, or Radovan Karadzic, the War Criminal *du jour.*

For someone to be considered inhuman, they must have done something that makes the rest of us cringe, thinking that we no longer identify with them or even perceive them to be members of the same species.

Which brings up an interesting, though often underappreciated truth:

> *Being human is a good thing*

In fact, God thought being human was such a good thing He decided to try it out Himself.

I want you to think about that for a moment: What you are is so good that God wanted to try it on for size. That's almost completely backwards from what most of us tend to think about humanity. Especially among Christians, it seems like the lowest common denominator of our faith is the belief that we should get off this rock, shuffle off this mortal coil, and reign somewhere up in the universe with God.

> But God comes here.

> God becomes like us.

> God loves human beings. God loves the world. Not an ideal human, but human beings as they are; not an ideal world, but the real world... while we exert ourselves to grow beyond our humanity, to leave the human behind us, God becomes human; and we must recognize that

> God wills that we be human...while we distinguish between pious and godless, good and evil, noble and base, God loves real people without distinction.
> **Dietrich Bonhoeffer**

By becoming human, Jesus saves us from our sin and restores us into right relationship with God. By becoming human, furthermore, Jesus shows us just how committed God is to being on the side of humanity.

He really is on our side.

This makes sense, given that Adam and Eve were made in the image of God (Genesis 1.27-28), and Paul describes Jesus as being the image of God (2 Corinthians 4.4).
>   This means that the thing we were meant to be—
>   human, made in God's image—
>   is the thing that Jesus actually is.

> The god of this age has blinded the minds of unbelievers, so that they cannot see the light of the gospel of the glory of Christ, who is the image of God.
> **2 Corinthians 4.4**

This, of course, doesn't mean that we become divine in the same way that Jesus was divine. In fact, it's worth noting here that all our attempts at equality with God so far have gone poorly.

> We ate from the Forbidden Tree in Eden, attempting to be like God, and losing our access to Paradise on Earth (Genesis 3).

> We built a tower in Babel to proclaim our Supremacy, only to lose the power to understand each another in the process (Genesis 11).

It does mean, however, that we can conform
>   to the image of Christ (Romans 8.29)
>   and have our true humanity restored (1 Corinthians 15.49).

>   It means that our humanization
>   is the only means to divinization we'll ever know.

If we follow along with Romans 5.12-21, we begin to understand that:

> Adam was made in the image of God, but sinned,
>> and so sin entered the world
>> and diminished the image of God.

> But Jesus Christ came as the image of God
>> and lived obediently, even into his atoning death,
>> which makes new life
>> and the restoration of the image of God
>>> available to all.

And here, then, is one of the most profound spiritual truths of all: the divine cannot be found apart from the human form. We only know God through Jesus. We only know what God is like through the life and times of Jesus of Nazareth, for he was God Himself living with us and as one of us.

> What the world needs today are ministers of the Gospel who are experts in humanity, who have a profound awareness of the heart of present-day men and women, participating in their joys and hopes, anguish and sadness, and who are at the same time contemplatives who have fallen in love with God. For this, we need new saints.
> **Pope John Paul II**

At this point, some might ask why this matters.

For starters, it matters because it teaches us to value the life we have here on earth.

> Your kingdom come,
> Your will be done
>> on earth as it is in heaven.
> **Matthew 6.10**

As a child I grew up around a lot of godly people who were very keen to escape earth and live forever in heaven. I couldn't help wondering, though, about whether or not heaven would be any more enjoyable for them than earth was. After all, the earth didn't really seem so bad to me, and the real issue seemed to be that some of these folks just didn't enjoy living.

And if that was the case, that living held no pleasure, then why would they want to live forever?

In the words of my Uncle Harry, an endearingly cantankerous old coot, to a bitter and difficult parishioner: *My dear, I pray you never die, because when you do you will certainly ruin the party in heaven with all your complaining.*

Ha!

Once we know that God loves humanity, that we are loved for being human, we can begin to appreciate the life we have now instead of lusting for the life we think we'll get later on.

Furthermore, knowing that Jesus came to restore the image of God within us, we can more fully invest in ourselves by working with the Spirit to excavate that image,
>   by being united with the fullness of God (Ephesians 3.19)
>   and sharing in the inheritance of the saints
>   in the light (Colossians 1.12)
>   as participants in the divine nature (2 Peter 1.3-4),
>   which, again, means becoming the kind of people
>   we were meant to be.

Lastly, knowing that our humanity matters is important because it reminds us that we are loved.

No matter what.

QUESTIONS FOR FURTHER REFLECTION

1. Can you think of a time when you heard someone referred to as being "inhuman?" What images come to your mind when you consider someone doing something in-humane? How do they make you feel?

2. Knowing that our humanity has been compromised by sin, reflect on the value of Jesus restoring the image of God to us. What do you imagine God perceives to be a true human being? How are you working with God to become more human?

PART TWO: KENOSIS

WE SERVE BECAUSE OF THE ONE WHO DESCENDED

Jesus, being God, descended from Heaven and came to live here. He gave up his divine privileges so, in honor of him, we should not rely on our earthly privileges. Because of the Incarnation we serve God and serve one another.

Your attitude should be the same as that of Christ Jesus:

Who, being in very nature God,
    did not consider equality with God
    something to be grasped,
But made himself nothing,
    taking the very nature of a servant,
    being made in human likeness.
And being found in appearance as a man,
    he humbled himself
    and became obedient to death—
        even death on a cross!

Therefore God exalted him to the highest place
    and gave him the name
    that is above every name,
        that at the name of Jesus
            every knee should bow,
                in heaven and on earth
                and under the earth,
            and every tongue confess
                that Jesus Christ is Lord,
                    to the glory of God
                    the Father.

Philippians 2.5-11

Dim dawn behind the tamerisks -- the sky is saffron-yellow --
As the women in the village grind the corn,
And the parrots seek the riverside, each calling to his fellow
That the Day, the staring Easter Day is born.
Oh the white dust on the highway! Oh the stenches in the byway!
Oh the clammy fog that hovers
And at Home they're making merry 'neath the white and scarlet berry --
What part have India's exiles in their mirth?

Full day begind the tamarisks -- the sky is blue and staring --
As the cattle crawl afield beneath the yoke,
And they bear One o'er the field-path, who is past all hope or caring,
To the ghat below the curling wreaths of smoke.
Call on Rama, going slowly, as ye bear a brother lowly --
Call on Rama -- he may hear, perhaps, your voice!
With our hymn-books and our psalters we appeal to other altars,
And to-day we bid "good Christian men rejoice!"

High noon behind the tamarisks -- the sun is hot above us --
As at Home the Christmas Day is breaking wan.
They will drink our healths at dinner -- those who tell us how they love us,
And forget us till another year be gone!
Oh the toil that knows no breaking! Oh the Heimweh, ceaseless, aching!
Oh the black dividing Sea and alien Plain!
Youth was cheap -- wherefore we sold it.
Gold was good -- we hoped to hold it,
And to-day we know the fulness of our gain.

Grey dusk behind the tamarisks -- the parrots fly together --
As the sun is sinking slowly over Home;
And his last ray seems to mock us shackled in a lifelong tether.
That drags us back how'er so far we roam.
Hard her service, poor her payment -- she is ancient, tattered raiment --
India, she the grim Stepmother of our kind.
If a year of life be lent her, if her temple's shrine we enter,
The door is hut -- we may not look behind.

Black night behind the tamarisks -- the owls begin their chorus --
As the conches from the temple scream and bray.
With the fruitless years behind us, and the hopeless years before us,
Let us honor, O my brother, Christmas Day!
Call a truce, then, to our labors -- let us feast with friends and neighbors,
And be merry as the custom of our caste;
For if "faint and forced the laughter," and if sadness follow after,
We are richer by one mocking Christmas past.

Christmas in India
Rudyard Kipling

THE 16STONE RUGBY MONSTER

Your attitude should be the same as that of Christ Jesus:

Who, being in very nature God,
    did not consider equality with God
    something to be grasped,
But made himself nothing,
    taking the very nature of a servant,
    being made in human likeness.
And being found in appearance as a man,
    he humbled himself
    and became obedient to death—
        even death on a cross!

Therefore God exalted him to the highest place
    and gave him the name
    that is above every name,
        that at the name of Jesus
            every knee should bow,
                in heaven and on earth
                and under the earth,
        and every tongue confess
            that Jesus Christ is Lord,
                to the glory of God
                the Father.

Philippians 2.5-11

When I coached rugby for little kids, one of my favorite parts was teaching them how to tackle. In rugby, the best way to tackle is to wrap your arms around your opponents' knees and squeeze them together. This, especially if you can grab your wrists on the other side of their legs to make a complete ring of contact fury, is a foolproof way to bring down even the hardiest foe.

In order to show the kids how to tackle this way, I'd get down on both knees and let them grab me, wrap my legs, and use the sides of their heads on the side of my hip to push me down.

Grab. Wrap. Push with the head.

Works every time.

Then, I'd get up on one knee and let them do it again.

Grab. Wrap. Push with the head.

Then, I'd get up to a full standing position and let them do it again.
Then I'd slowly run and let them come at me from an angle.

Grab. Wrap. Push with the head.

Then I'd move faster and faster so they got the hang of tackling a 16stone monster every single time up and down the pitch.

For them, and for me, it was always glorious.

We used to scrimmage, too. Of course, in the scrimmage I'd not use the full measure of my weight and speed against the little kids. Often, the coaches would make a rule that forced us (the coaching staff) to tie one hand behind our backs; or, with the wee little ones, we'd tie both legs together and make ourselves hop.

We gave up all our advantages.

Naturally, we could have cheated, quickly untying our hands or legs, or using our full strength and speed...but we didn't want to. It wasn't like we were disabled, we just limited ourselves because we loved those kids and it was fun to play with them.

Do you see where I'm going with this?

Jesus Christ was fully God but came to the earth to live as a man, divesting himself of his divine privilege—which, by the way, doesn't mean he wasn't God anymore, just that he deliberately set aside the full measure of his power, refusing to access it though he could have at any moment, because he loved us and chose to live among us as a man.

Jesus was the 16stone rugby monster in the scrimmage of humanity.

> He added to himself which he was not, he did not lose what he was.
> **St. Augustine**

> He assumed the form of a servant without the defilement of sin, enriching what was human, not impairing what was divine.
> **Leo the Great**

> The decision was not to stop being divine. It was a decision about what it meant to be divine.
> **N.T. Wright**

Again, Jesus became human but did not lose his divine attributes. Paul's first letter to Timothy makes this exceedingly clear, referring to Jesus' eternality, immortality, invisibility ,and divinity (1.17). Additionally, while he was alive, the Scriptures testify to Jesus' being omnipresent (Matthew 28.20), omnipotent (John 1.3), the Savior of the World (Philippians 2.10-11), and divine (Luke 1-2).

As a parent, I'm often struck by how different our self-emptying God is from pretty much anyone, or anything, else. For example, when my kids misbehave I discipline them—lovingly, of course, but still I use my authority as their father and my near-limitless power to control television, video games, and toys.

My kids listen because I make them.

But I know that they only listen half-heartedly. They still bicker when I'm not around. They don't like to share. They aren't keen on a healthy balance between constructive play and mindless entertainment, let alone between nutritious meals and fun snacks.

My kids just do what kids do.

And so I find myself imagining what it would be like to incarnate myself as a child, to come into their lives as a supposed brother, a 7-year old David

McDonald. I think I could model for them what a life of love and friendship, sharing and togetherness, could look like...because I'd be living that life as an example based on my identity as their father.

I know better, and I could show them a better way if I was one of them instead of just being their loving-yet-authoritative father.

God doesn't just make us listen. He comes to us as one of us. He is with us. He knows. He understands. He could have come into the world as a tyrant, as a king, as a political figure, or as a war hero. Instead, He chose to come as one of the working poor, living in occupied territory, surrounded by scandal and accusation, living in relative obscurity in the middle of nowhere.

The word that describes God emptying Himself through the Incarnation is called *kenosis*.

It was God's *kenotic* love that allowed Him to empty Himself and come down to earth.

In actual fact, God's love is doubly *kenotic*, because He did not merely come down to earth, but He came down to the lowest portion of earth. He retained neither heavenly privilege nor earthly position.

He not only became a man, He became a man most of us would ignore. There's a touch of revolution in that maneuver, a little indictment to remind us that the whole world is upside down anyway.

> The Incarnation is not a destructive, aggressive act of invasion in which sinful humanity is battered into submission; it is an act of enticement in which the love of God is shown, and the love of humanity is elicited in response. God enters our world to make it known—and make it possible—that we can enter His world, not as gatecrashers or invaders, but as welcome guests.
> **Allister McGrath**

In our world it always seems that might makes right, but that is one of the chief errors that Christ came to reverse (Mark 10.43-45). When we love and serve Jesus, we find true power and authority by emptying ourselves of our privileges, becoming the servant of all, so as to be elevated before God.

If anyone wants to be first, he must be the very last, and the servant of all.
Mark 9.35

We must learn to divest ourselves of privilege in this world,
      cooperating with the Spirit to rely on God
            instead of on ourselves.

      This means putting our security
            in something other than a 401(k),
      putting our hopes
            in something other than good government,
      putting our trust
            in something other than our shared values.

      Because financial security is a privilege,
            and we should be thankful we have it,
      but in the end it won't save our souls.

      Because good government is a privilege,
            and we should be thankful we have it,
      but in the end it won't create lasting peace.

      Because good values and shared ideals are privileges,
            and we should be thankful we have them,
      but in the end they will not guarantee
            our ongoing transformation
            into the kind of people
               God intends for us to become,
      nor will they ensure vitality and love
            in all our relationships,
               no matter how hard we try.

At some point, all privileges are exposed for what they truly are: fleeting.

When we live in privilege,
      we start to believe that our privileges
            count for more than they really do,
            and that they'll last longer than they really will,
               and that they are more essential
               than they actually are.

So, like Christ Jesus, we must learn to put our privileges aside. That doesn't mean we should blow our wealth or protest against our national security; it just means we need to get into the discipline of confessing and believing that our wealth and security are truly found in something other than in this world.

> Do not store up for yourselves treasures on earth, where moth and rust destroy, and where thieves break in and steal. But store up for yourselves treasures in heaven, where moth and rust do not destroy, and where thieves do not break in and steal.
> **Matthew 6.19-20**

My friend Ting took this to an extreme I could not possibly have imagined. Coming from a wealthy family in his native Hong Kong, Ting moved to Canada to study medicine at the University of British Columbia. He went to school between September and May, but in the off months he did something way out of the ordinary.

He lived as a homeless person.

Understand, Ting had more money at his disposal than most small independent states, but he believed strongly in his brotherhood with the indigent, the disadvantaged, and the outcast.

Because of how he lived during those few years of Medical school, Ting went on to become one of the best doctors and most compassionate people I've ever met. He knew he was privileged, but he refused to ride on that privilege. He set it aside so he could more fully invest himself in helping and serving others, so that he could live among them.

Like Christ.

QUESTIONS FOR FURTHER REFLECTION

1. Do you resonate with the idea of the Incarnation as being like playing sports with little kids? Does it make sense to you that God would limit Himself in this way in order to live among us? What does that tell you about the nature of God.

2. Take a moment and either write or converse about how Jesus retained his divinity while taking on humanity. Of the Scriptures listen in support of this truth, which one do you find most compelling? Which one makes the most sense to you? It may be worthwhile to underline that verse in your Bible, or maybe to write it in your journal or somewhere you're likely to see it regularly.

3. What does *kenosis* mean?

4. What does it mean for us to empty ourselves of our privileges like Jesus emptied himself of his divine privileges? Is there a danger in taking this too far? Or, is the danger in not taking this far enough? How can you tell?

SUCK IT UP AND SERVE THE LORD

A few years ago I was in La Roche, Haiti with some friends to do some humanitarian aid. It was a pretty grueling experience, given that our chief task for the first few days was to wade into a clogged septic pit and shovel it out. Truthfully, we didn't know in advance that's what we'd be doing. We thought we'd be feeding starving children or doing interviews with Sally Struthers... either one of which would've been preferable to the big crappy mess we found ourselves in.

My friend, Chris, didn't flinch though. Instead, he looked at me and said something I'll never forget: *It's time to suck it up and serve the Lord.*

That phrase went on to become a catchphrase for us, invoked whenever we had to do something unpleasant—either for work, for church, for family, or in ministry.

Because, sometimes, we have to go into the heart of the suck to sort out the things that really matter to God, to others, to ourselves, and to the world.

Like septic tanks.

In Haiti.

Anyway, this understanding of Christian service is pretty crucial to following the way of Jesus, especially given that our whole world works in almost the exact opposite way. Our world is about privilege and luxury and position. It's about wealth—the accumulation of wealth and the accumulation of goods and comfort—but the way of Jesus is not about any of those things. The way of Jesus is not about blessing. The way of Jesus is about suffering, servitude, and solidarity. The way of Jesus is about doing things that are not always pleasant, and recognizing—understanding—that you're cooperating with God and healing the world as you do.

Much of how we understand this idea of servitude is grounded in the Book of Isaiah. Isaiah was a prophet who lived several hundred years before the time of Christ in occupied Assyrian territory. Isaiah spoke prophetically about a character called The Servant. Thanks to Handel's *Messiah* and thanks, of course, to the work of the Apostle Paul, we understand this person to be Jesus.

> He was despised and rejected by men,
>> a man of sorrows
>> and familiar with suffering.
>
> Surely he took up our infirmities
>> and carried our sorrows,
>>> yet we considered him stricken by God,
>>> smitten by him and afflicted.
>
> But he was pierced for our transgressions,
>> he was crushed for our iniquities;
>>> the punishment that brought us peace
>>>> was upon him
>>> and by his stripes we are healed.
>
> After the suffering of his soul,
>> he will see the light of life and be satisfied;
>>> by his knowledge my righteous servant
>>> will justify many
>>> and he will bear their iniquities.

Isaiah 53.3-5, 11

Isaiah is telling us the person who faithfully serves God will suffer for serving. It is not empty suffering, though, but redemptive suffering. It's a kind of deviance in the face of evil, in the face of overwhelming odds. It says: *Go ahead, do your worst. I will not quit, I will not lie down, because my suffering has a purpose.* It means the person who wants to faithfully serve God does not just get job perks, or little bonuses, or a special platform to be famous. The person who wants to faithfully serve God will suffer.

Are you getting this? Following God always involves some measure of sacrifice and suffering, even if you happen to be His son.

Every time we act as advocates, as shadows, as imitators of God, every time God uses us to be heroic in some way, to sacrifice in some way, it really is a sacrifice. It's not a little basketball-high-school-movie sacrifice. It's a real sacrifice that will cost you something—it's going to hurt. We understand this because the greatest of us, Jesus himself, paid a wicked penalty for his heroism and for our salvation.

It costs something to follow the ways of God.
It costs something to advocate for others.
It costs something to serve others.
     And yet Jesus shows us the way forward.

     The way forward involves suffering;
          it involves service.

The way to be human is to serve other humans. The way to be a person is through other people. If you want to discover your humanity, it will be found in the way you treat others.

     Whoever humbles himself will be exalted.
     Matthew 23:12

If you want to follow Jesus, you have to serve. You have to serve others and you have to serve God. You have to serve the concerns of God, the mission of God, and the mission of Christ. You have to love others.

Let's see, how else can I say this to hammer it in?

I always get hesitant when I start speaking so directly, because I imagine some cynical readers have already had their fill of my cutesy "serve Jesus" talk.

But they don't get it.

If you don't want to follow in the way of Jesus, do whatever you want, but you won't be a participant in anything I'm talking about.

If you want to follow Jesus then serve—because that's what he did, because that's what he commanded us to do, because that's the way he makes his kingdom real, present, manifest, obvious. That's the way he sets up kingdom franchises in our hearts—by loving all, by serving others, by serving him.

> It's hard,
>> but it's worth it.
> It's humbling,
>> but humility is central to the way of Jesus.
> It feels mindless,
>> but that should encourage you
>> to fill your mind with thoughts of Christ
>>> and with prayer.

Jesus came into this world as a servant to demonstrate that progress for humanity does not involve a mad panic and a lust of power. Instead, the world works best through mutuality and submission, through love and service, through authenticating and valuing others before oneself.

> For even the Son of Man came not to be served, but to serve, and to give His life as a ransom for many.
> **Mark 10.45**

> The last shall be first, and the first shall be last.
> **Mark 10.31**

Even knowing that the very people he had come to save would betray and abandon him, Jesus demonstrated the value of servitude right up until his last episode with the disciples. In John 13, we read about the Last Supper, which begins with Jesus washing the feet of his followers and instructing them to do likewise.

Jesus, King of the Universe, came into the world to serve. Those who find their greatest connection with God through service do so because of the example of Christ.

Regardless of our status in life, we must all learn to serve others, because Jesus came to live among us as a servant.

QUESTIONS FOR FURTHER REFLECTION

1. When was the last time you had to "suck it up and serve the Lord?" What value was there in that experience? Did you feel like that was going to be valuable at the time? Or, did it take a while for you to realize the good that you had done? Who helped you understand this?

2. How different, really, do you think the way of Jesus – of suffering, servitude, and solidarity – really is from the way of the world? Is this difference exaggerated sometimes? By whom? And, for what purpose? How do you imagine Jesus would live if he were alive in the world today?

3. Take a moment and brainstorm with some of your friends and family the places where you might serve, or the people you might volunteer with. What do these people and these places have in common? What do you they have to teach you?

dr. david mcdonald

RED PLASTIC CUP

I get together every week with my friend Greg for some spiritual coaching. Greg is a brilliant man and a solid businessman, so I consider it a high honor to serve as his spiritual advisor. Every week we get together and every week Greg brings this red plastic cup. It's not much to look at—just some Costco-looking thing that probably gets sold 100-for-$1, like an ecological grenade on sale at Munitions-R-Us—but Greg treats it like his prized possession.

So we've started to use it to illustrate several of our talking points.

In particular, we've used this cup to talk about the value of Christians because of Christ living inside us. Imagine, for example, pouring liquid gold into the crummy red plastic cup. Because of what's inside the cup, despite its outward appearance, that cup is now pretty valuable.

We are like this cup. As we've discovered in earlier chapters, we're not worthy of God's affection on our own, but since we've been filled with the Spirit of Christ, our value has been immeasurably increased.

> We have this treasure in jars of clay to show that this all-surpassing power is from God and not from us.
> **2 Corinthians 4.7**

No matter who you are or what you've done, you need to understand that you have great value in this world (and to the God who made it) because you are full of the Spirit.

> Those who are led by the Spirit of God are sons of God.
> **Romans 8.14**

And this central truth doesn't just concern our value to God, but also our ability to make a difference in the lives of others. Even the weakest of us is made powerful in him.

> [God's] grace is sufficient for you, for [His] power is made perfect in weakness.
> **2 Corinthians 12.9**

Christ was born into this world so he could be born again in us.
    Just as he was born in a stable
            in a manger
            in Bethlehem
            in the darkness
                    and without any real protection in the world,
    so, too, he is born again in the brokenness
            and stupidity
                    of our mistakes
                    and our guilt
                    and our messy relationships
            and in the darkness of our addictions,
                    without any real protection
                            from family
                            or government
                                    or perfect earthly circumstance.

God has made His home in the hearts of those who don't belong,
        who are rejected because they're weak,
        who are discredited because they're incompetent,
            and who are tortured because they've failed.

He makes his home in us,
        living in the red plastic cup of our heart,

                    and so elevating
                    and redeeming
                            our worthlessness,
                            restoring our value.

As he does this for us, we should bear in mind that he willingly did this for others, too. So our attitude towards those whose reddish plasticity is particularly distasteful should be gracious, loving, gentle, and kind.

> Religion that God our Father accepts as pure and faultless is this: to look after orphans and widows in their distress and to keep oneself from being polluted by the world.
> **James 1.27**

> Give fair judgment to the poor man, the afflicted, the fatherless, the destitute. Rescue the poor and helpless from the grasp of evil men.
> **Psalm 82:3**

On my most recent trip to Africa, I was privileged to meet a woman named Mamma Mary, a sort-of matriarch for some of the rural townships outside of Pretoria. Mamma Mary is very poor and has very little in the way of possessions, but you would be a fool to judge her on the basis of her red plastic cup.

She has been awarded the title Mamma Africa by the South African government, a title shared only by Miriam Makeba (the famous singer) and Winnie Madikizela-Mandela (the second wife of Nelson Mandela). She has started four orphanages, though she insists they be called "children's villages" in order to avoid scarring the children or labeling them destructively at an impressionable age, and she has devoted herself to the wellbeing of her community.

When I sat in Mamma Mary's dining room—eating chicken feet no less—I heard her rattle off the single most impressive theological discourse since Christ himself. She spoke eloquently about people being made in God's image, and sharply about how that image is damaged when we refuse to treat other people as they should be treated. We damage God's image in others when we refuse them personhood, and we damage His image in us when we diminish anything in God's creation.

She told me that, in a house made out of concrete blocks in one of the poorest places in the universe, while eating chicken feet and holding my hand.

You cannot judge another person by what they look like, or where they come from. You can only look at them and ask the Spirit to show you that they—like you—are filled with God's liquid gold.

QUESTIONS FOR FURTHER REFLECTION

1. Reflect briefly on the illustration of the red plastic cup filled with liquid gold. Does this make sense to you? Does it help you better understand your value to God? Does it make you feel less valuable? If so, do you think that may be because some of your value is located in the wrong place (i.e. in having a beautiful golden cup, filled only with water)? How can you ensure that you find value in the right place in your life?

2. Who do you know that has a particularly reddish plasticity? Who do you know that needs someone to see their inherent value as a child of God? How can you show them you love them, and value them, as God loves and values them?

3. Has anyone ever shown you love regardless of whether or not you deserved it? How did that make you feel? How do you think it made them feel?

down to earth

PART THREE: MISSION

WE GO BECAUSE OF THE ONE WHO CAME

Jesus came to save the world. His mission has now become our mission. Because of the Incarnation, it is the task of the church to heal the world.

For God so loved the world that he gave his one and only Son, that whoever believes in him shall not perish but have eternal life. For God did not send his Son into the world to condemn the world, but to save the world through him.

John 3.16-17

FROM THE WORD

South of the Line, inland from far Durban,
A mouldering soldier lies--your countryman.
Awry and doubled up are his gray bones,
And on the breeze his puzzled phantom moans
Nightly to clear Canopus: "I would know
By whom and when the All-Earth-gladdening Law
Of Peace, brought in by that Man Crucified,
Was ruled to be inept, and set aside?

And what of logic or of truth appears
In tacking 'Anno Domini' to the years?
Near twenty-hundred livened thus have hied,
But tarries yet the Cause for which He died."

A Christmas Ghost Story
Thomas Hardy

SAVE 'EM AND TAKE 'EM

For God so loved the world that he gave his one and only Son, that whoever believes in him shall not perish but have eternal life. For God did not send his Son into the world to condemn the world, but to save the world through him.

John 3.16-17

The creation waits in eager expectation for the sons of God to be revealed. For the creation was subjected to frustration, not by its own choice, but by the will of the one who subjected it, in hope that the creation itself will be liberated from its bondage to decay and brought into the glorious freedom of the children of God. We know that the whole creation has been groaning as in the pains of childbirth right up to the present time.

Romans 8.19-22

Ever see a movie where the hero spends the first ninety minutes of the film chasing after his ultimate goal, and then—through some weird, inexplicable snobby art-house reason—the movie just ends without the main storyline even being addressed?

Or, perhaps even more common, have you ever seen a movie where the central conflict is never even presented? Where you realize, about half-way through, that you have no idea what this movie is really about?

Have you seen *Transformers* 2?

Any of the next-gen *Star Wars* (including the animated feature, though not
the weekly cartoon...it's quite solid)?

Or any of the *Jaws,*
     Rambo,
     Scary Movie,
     Saw,
          or *Friday 13ᵗʰ* films?

These movies amble, like 24-frame-per-second zombies, across the cinescape while their producers dance to the soft ruffle of my $20 bill as it lands in the concession till.

The movies aren't clear and because they aren't clear they aren't compelling. Furthermore, their lack of clarity isn't about some purported mystery—it's just poor storytelling.

I'm getting to the point.

Jesus, thankfully, had a clearer end in mind than either Uwe Boll or Michael Bay did with their movies. In fact, Jesus was crystal clear about why he Incarnated: *to save the world.*

> I did not come to judge the world, but to save it.
> **John 12.47**

> I have come to give you life, life abundant.
> **John 10.10**

The doctrine of the Incarnation is really about God acting in Jesus for the salvation of all the world. From the beginning, this was the reason for Christ coming into the world.

It was a rescue operation.

And, since there are still obviously parts of the world that need healing— spiritual healing for those caught in sin, ecological healing for the planet, sociological and political healing for those in developing nations, financial healing for those suffering in the global economic collapse—we are called to take Jesus' Great Commission seriously.

> All authority in heaven and on earth has been given to me. Therefore go and make disciples of all nations, baptizing them in the name of the Father and of the Son and of the Holy Spirit, and teaching them to obey everything I have commanded you.
> **Matthew 28.18-20**

And this rescue mission is not just about saving souls—though it is indeed about saving souls through participating in the gospel message of Jesus Christ—but equally about healing the world. All creation groans in expectation of the time when God will make things right (Romans 8.22), and even now eagerly awaits our cooperation with the Spirit to begin what God will ultimately complete (Romans 8.19-20).

We must accept Jesus' enlistment into the Great Commission and cooperate with his Spirit in healing the world. Otherwise, what good are we? If we are not going to work with God towards the redemption of the world, then why are we here? If God just wanted to save us, He'd save us and then kill us off one by one so He could more quickly enjoy our company in Heaven.

Right?

But since we're still breathing—and, in your case, reading—it's safe to assume that we have been saved for a purpose.

And the purpose is to cooperate with God in healing the world.
The purpose is to fulfill the mission of Jesus.

There are those who would object. My maternal grandmother, Jetta Doss, was one. She was a saint, but she had a pretty low view of this world. And, joking aside, she did pray regularly for her children and grandchildren that God would "save 'em and take 'em, " so they couldn't accidently backslide and lose their salvation.

Well, Granny Doss was a lot of good things, but she was no theologian.

We're saved for something,
not just from something.

We're saved so we can shadow God
        and heal the world,
    not just so we don't live through Hell on earth
        before landing someplace worse.

> God enlists you and me and all of us to be His fellow workers, agents for transfiguration, to transform, transfigure all the ugliness of this world, to help God realize His dream so that the kingdoms of this world would become the Kingdom of our God and his Christ and he shall reign for ever and ever. Amen.
> **Desmond Tutu**

Make no mistake, there are plenty of sincere Christians who have allowed themselves to be unmoved by Jesus' mission. They are like the Scribes in Matthew 2 who know where the Messiah will be born but neglect to go with the wise men. They know that the infinite has entered the finite, but are too comfortable to go and see.

The couch is always the foil to the cross.

Each of us, everyday, must remember why Christ came and what share we have in his mission to heal the world.

The alternative is to have Granny Doss pray for you.

QUESTIONS FOR FURTHER REFLECTION

1. What was the mission of Jesus? Why should this mission now be our mission? In what ways can we cooperate with him in healing the world?

2. What do you think are your greatest obstacles to more faithfully sharing the gospel with other people? Can you think of any times when you've shared this message and had it feel "right?" What can you do to ensure those opportunities appear with greater frequency in your life? What kind of prayers should you be praying in order for God to help you work with Him?

PARACHUTE BROTHERS AND HOUDINI SISTER:

Rob Bell makes a great point in his book *Jesus Wants to Save Christians*—he says that God needs a body.

Citing God's instruction to Moses, when God told him he would be like God to Pharaoh (Exodus 7.1), Rob says:

> God needs skin and bones so that Pharaoh will know just who this God is he's dealing with and how this God acts in the world. And this is not just so Pharaoh will know but so that all of humanity will know (p 31).

What was true then is true now: God needs a body.

And, of course, He still has one for we are the body of Christ.

> Just as each of us has one body with many members, and these members do not all have the same function, so in Christ we who are many form one body, and each member belongs to all the others.
> **Romans 12.4-5**

The body is a unit, though it is made up of many parts; and though all

its parts are many, they form one body. So it is with Christ. For we were all baptized by one Spirit into one body...
1 Corinthians 12.12-13

... Christ is the head of the church, his body, of which he is the Savior.
Ephesians 5.23b

[Christ] is the head of the body, the church...
Colossians 1.18

Whenever we continue cooperating with God to heal the world, acting as God's shadows and emissaries within it, we are acting as the hands and feet of Jesus.

Do you see what this means?

We continue the Incarnation.

The real Presence of God in the World did not end with the Ascension of Jesus Christ, for Christ is still alive and working in the world through us, his body, his church. He is present whenever his mission is being carried out. As such, the Incarnation was not the whole of his coming, but merely the beginning.

You are still in the process of your coming.
Karl Rahner

In the beginning,
God created us to be His stewards for all the world.
We mucked that up pretty good.

Now, in the new beginning
available to those lovers and followers of Jesus Christ,
God has once again entrusted us with His creation,
He has charged us with healing the world
we neglected to preserve.

Once again we see that God always works toward the same purpose—both in the beginning and now, again, in the new beginning: looking after His creation.

And this purpose is the same as Jesus' purpose, for Jesus was sent by the Father (John 6.57, 13) and acts on His behalf (John 5.30), which means he and the Father are united (John 17.20-25).

Jesus made the Word flesh, and now the task of the Church is to make the Word concrete—to demonstrate the veracity of Christ's mission so the world can clearly understand the love of God and His mission to save.

There are a disappointingly large number of Christians, though, who want nothing to do with the Church. Their rationale is that the contemporary church has little to do with the church as its revealed in the Second Testament, and so they have looked elsewhere for Christian community, edification, instruction, and fellowship.

This is sad.

While it is true that the contemporary church has its flaws—and I am well aware of those flaws—it's also true that the church in the Second Testament had its flaws too. One need only read 1 + 2 Corinthians, or the letters to the Seven Churches in Revelation (2-3), to understand just how deeply flawed they were.

And the truth is the Church will always be terribly flawed. Karl Barth reminds us of our earliest heritage when he noted that the first church had three people—*one good, two bad, one of whom became good*—founded when Christ died on Calvary with two murderous thieves.

Churches will always be full of murderous thieves, but some of them will actually experience Jesus and be transformed by him.

one good, two bad, one of whom became good

By leaving the Church, my parachute-brothers and Houdini-sisters do us (and themselves) great harm, for they are now doubly-removed, as my friend Jvo puts it. They are removed from the world by virtue of being saved, but they are also removed from the Church by virtue of their distaste for murderous thieves.

I understand their distaste. I share it.

But I can never forget that Christ died between two bad men,
    one of whom *became good*.

And so I can never leave his Church, even when it's obviously not turning out precisely as he instructed.

No matter how you slice it, the Church—with all its flaws and phoniness—matters to God.

Christ died for the Church.

Our chief obligation, then, to this Church—his Body—is to ensure that we stay focused on the mission of God to heal the world. We must work tirelessly to ensure that this remains our focus.

We are here, as regents and stewards, viceroys and idols, to ensure that God's will is done on earth as it is in heaven.

We are here to incarnate the Incarnation, to continue the work Christ himself began, in anticipation of God's ultimate intervention and the rescue of Creation.

That is what it means to be the Church.

QUESTIONS FOR FURTHER REFLECTION

1. Reflect briefly on the statement God needs a body. What does that mean to you? How do you understand that in terms of Moses standing before Pharaoh? In terms of Jesus' Incarnation? In terms of the mission of the Church? In what ways are you, personally, the hands and feet of Jesus?

2. Take a moment and look up each of the Scriptures contained within this chapter that pertain to the Church as the Body of Christ. Look at their surrounding context, the handful of verses before and after them. What similarities do you notice between them? What differences? How do you reconcile these?

3. What do you make of the assertion that the Church is the continuing Incarnation of Jesus? How does that change your understanding of church? Does that cause you to reevaluate your role within your local church? Why? Or, why not?

4. When was the last time you felt so disappointed in church that you considered leaving for good? Did you? If so, does reading this chapter challenge you to re-engage? If not, what made you stay? Has staying positively or negatively affected your spiritual journey? In what ways?

LEAVE THE LAMB ALONE

While Paul was waiting for them in Athens, he was greatly distressed to see that the city was full of idols. So he reasoned in the synagogue with the Jews and the God-fearing Greeks, as well as in the marketplace day by day with those who happened to be there. A group of Epicurean and Stoic philosophers began to dispute with him. Some of them asked, "What is this babbler trying to say?" Others remarked, "He seems to be advocating foreign gods." They said this because Paul was preaching the good news about Jesus and the resurrection. Then they took him and brought him to a meeting of the Areopagus, where they said to him, "May we know what this new teaching is that you are presenting? You are bringing some strange ideas to our ears, and we want to know what they mean." (*All the Athenians and the foreigners who lived there spent their time doing nothing but talking about and listening to the latest ideas.*)

Paul then stood up in the meeting of the Areopagus and said: "Men of Athens! I see that in every way you are very religious. For as I walked around and looked carefully at your objects of worship, I even found an altar with this inscription: TO AN UNKNOWN GOD. Now what you worship as something unknown I am going to proclaim to you.

"The God who made the world and everything in it is the Lord of heaven and earth and does not live in temples built by hands. And he is not served by human hands, as if he needed anything, because he himself gives all men life and breath and everything else. From one man he made every nation of men, that they should inhabit the whole earth; and he determined the times set for them and the exact places where they should live. God did this so that men would seek him and perhaps reach out for him and find him, though he is not far from each one of us. 'For in him we live and move and have our being.' As some of your own poets have said, 'We are his offspring.'

"Therefore since we are God's offspring, we should not think that the divine being is like gold or silver or stone—an image made by man's design and skill. In the past God overlooked such ignorance, but now he commands all people everywhere to repent. For he has set a day when he will judge the world with justice by the man he has appointed. He has given proof of this to all men by raising him from the dead."

When they heard about the resurrection of the dead, some of them sneered, but others said, "We want to hear you again on this subject." At that, Paul left the Council. A few men became followers of Paul and believed. Among them was Dionysius, a member of the Areopagus, also a woman named Damaris, and a number of others.
Acts 17.16-34

I used to hide my science fiction novels from my parents.

And my Guns n' Roses t-shirt (in my pillow case, no less).

It wasn't that these things were strictly *verboten*, just that I had a strong understanding that my folks weren't too keen on worldly music or magical fiction.

I understand why—after all, good parents want to protect their children from the mental, emotional, and spiritual harm—but I often think they missed out on something, too.

Faced with a world that most certainly contained a kind of spiritual plague, my parents decided to shelter me almost entirely from its influence. I went to church three times a week, was enrolled in Christian school, went to Christian camps, and became a leader in my church youth group.

I'm not going to criticize their approach. Actually, I'm quite grateful for the kind of people my parents were (and are). And, after all, I ended up a pastor. So somehow their protective posture was proven to be effective in keeping me connected to Jesus.

But, again, I grew up thinking that the run-and-hide mentality toward culture was weird, somehow off-balance. When I would talk with my "non-Christian" friends, I often felt like I was speaking another language. They didn't always understand what I was talking about, or why I cared *so much* about certain things (like Israel, or homosexuality, or swearing). Speaking with "normal" people required constant translation, forcing me to become culturally bi-lingual.

I knew English, and also a language many of us came to call Christian-ese.

(I've often wondered, by the way, if that moniker is somehow offensive to people who speak other –ese languages, like Japanese, for example).

It all came to a head for me when my Indian (as in, from India) friend Steve visited my church with me. Ignorant of precisely how different Christian-ese was from normal human talk, I neglected to prepare Steve for what he was about to experience. And, since I was leading worship that day, I had no way to give Steve the play-by-play during church.

Which made me feel really bad when he left half-way through the music looking terrified.

Fortunately, Steve only retreated to the lobby and I was able to catch up with him after the singing was over. I asked him what was wrong, and he looked at me with panicky terror in his eyes and said: *Why are you hurting the lamb? Why can't you people just leave the lamb alone?*

...

...

> The lamb?

And then it hit me: We were singing about Jesus Christ as a sacrificial lamb, "slain for the sins of the world", but we'd never explained the metaphor. Steve thought we were singing songs about murdering farm animals.

I laughed, and then explained what was going on. I walked Steve through the First Testament instructions about propitiation and the remission of sin, further explicating how Christ became the ultimate sacrifice for the sins of the world. It was a long conversation, but a good one. Some lights came on for him.

But only after I'd translated Christian-ese to human.

Christian doctrine requires translation, from something complicated and theological into something Steve can understand.

Every translator knows you've got to be spot on in both languages, with idioms and colloquialisms galore, in order to faithfully share what's being communicated.

This means we've got to:
1. know our Christian doctrine backwards and forwards; and
2. know the common parlance of our times inside and out; so we can
3. translate from the one to the other

There is biblical precedent for this.

In Acts 17, the Apostle Paul begins to share the gospel of God with the philosophers of Athens using Greek poetry. Normally, Paul would have used Hebrew Scripture as his raw material for talking about Jesus Christ, but Paul understood what I did not.

The people had no clue what the Scriptures said, so sharing Christ via the Scriptures would have been futile. Instead, Paul used their "scripture" and translated the message of Jesus into the language of his audience.

> I have become all things to all men so that by all possible means I might save some.
> **1 Corinthians 9.22b**

If Paul had simply retreated from the culture, he could not have spoken so eloquently about Jesus in a way the philosophers could understand. He had to know their stuff so he could share Jesus' stuff.

Which brings me back to science fiction novels and Guns n' Roses. That's the stuff Steve understood, and was—in fact—the raw materials I used in the church lobby to translate propitiation out of sheep-massacre.

My parents didn't rob me of anything by isolating me from culture; but I had to learn the value of inculturating the gospel (translating the message of Jesus from Chrisitan-ese to human) from someone else.

I learned it from reading Tom Beaudion, author of *Virtual Faith*. I've never met Tom, but his book affected me deeply because in it he shares how he moved from a posture of cultural-isolation to one of engagement for the sake of the Gospel. Tom was a former priest who became a high school teacher. He was deeply frustrated by his students' lack of concern for anything other than movies, music, girls (or guys) and video games.

He claims it took a long time for him to understand that God had placed him in that school to teach the students to care.

He claims it took an even longer time for him to understand that he would have to speak the students' language, not force them to learn Thomas Aquinas or St. Thomas Moore.

So Tom began to translate the Gospel of God into the language of pop culture, of movies, music, and video games.

I read this book shortly after my experience with Steve and a light-bulb shaped tongue-of-fire appeared over my head: I had to speak in a new tongue, a new language, one that all the Steves in the world could understand.

The heart of the Incarnation is about God going out of His way to speak human, not forcing us to behave but living among us in weakness and poverty so that we know He's on our side. In the way that Jesus emptied himself and lived with us, we have to empty ourselves of our religious privilege—our affection for doctrine and dogma spun out in Christian-ese—and learn to speak human.

The Incarnation teaches us about the importance of contextualization.
> God placed Himself in our context.
> We need to place ourselves in context of the world.

> I have sent them into the world
> **John 17.18**

In Acts 2 we read about a fascinating experience on the Day of Pentecost. On that day, after gathering for 120 days of prayerful waiting for the Spirit, Jesus' followers are baptized with fire:

> Suddenly a sound like the blowing of a violent wind came from heaven and filled the whole house where they were sitting. They saw what

seemed to be tongues of fire that separated and came to rest on each of them. All of them were filled with the Holy Spirit and began to speak in other tongues as the Spirit enabled them.

Acts 2.2-4

The result of this miraculous phenomenon? People from all over the world heard about the wonders of God in a language they could understand (2.11), and Peter was able to spend time teaching and explaining to them God's desire to heal the world and save humanity (2.14-40).

About three thousand people began to follow Jesus Christ that day, because they could make sense of the Gospel (2.40).

After the arrival of the Holy Spirit at Pentecost God's people were convinced that engaging the world around them was important, even though at times it meant giving up their religious preferences and privilege (Acts 10.9-29). As a result, people were saved, churches were planted, cultures were redeemed and the Holy Spirit increasingly began working in God's people to advance His Kingdom.

As lovers and followers of Jesus Christ,
> we are charged with engaging the culture around us,
> with contextualizing the Gospel message
>> so people can hear it in a way that makes sense to them.

> We are charged with loving and serving others,
>> with working towards personal
>>> and interpersonal
>> transformation,
>> teaching others
>>> (as we, ourselves, are further taught)
>> about the way of Jesus
>>> and his mission to heal the world.

That's Incarnational ministry:
> engagement,
> context,
> relationship,
> transformation,
> teaching,
>> and mission.

That's how Jesus "did ministry."
>He engaged the world.
>He entered into the context of humanity.
>He loved and served others.
>He worked tirelessly to see spiritual transformation in his followers.
>He taught, through a variety of mediums, about the Kingdom.
>He gave his life to save the world.

:: engagement :: context :: relationships ::

:: transformation :: teaching :: mission ::

Sometimes, though, we go the other route.
>In contrast to Incarnational ministry,
>>we find ourselves bludgeoning others
>>>with religion and Scripture,
>>with loveless charity
>>>fueled by denominational guilt,
>>with domineering colonization
>>>(and, sadly, this is often accompanied by violence in the name
>>>>of God),
>>with self-empowerment
>>>instead of self-emptying,
>>with isolation and protection from the world
>>>instead of engagement with it,

and so on...

Maybe these aren't the greatest sins in the universe, but they certainly are divergent from the way of Jesus and the movement of God's Spirit, both in Scripture and in us.

We are here to look for what's best in the world,
>to affirm it,
>>to see Christ transform and complete it,
>>>and to translate
>>>>the good news
>>>>of his coming
>>>>>so everyone can know God.

QUESTIONS FOR FURTHER REFLECTION

1. What are some of the positive effects of sheltering our children from the world? What are some of the negative effects? How should we strike a balance between the two – for, certainly, a child is less prepared to "be inculturated" than an adult? Who do you know that can help you navigate this tension in real life?

2. "Christian-ese" is a fairly common term used by Christians to describe the way we speak. Think of some examples of Christian-ese and talk about them with your friends or satellite group. Where have these words/phrases come from? How do you think "non-Christians" would hear them? Can you imagine your friends and family coming to church and having an experience similar to that of Steve and the lamb? If they did, would you be equipped to talk them through it afterwards? If not, what should you be doing to become equipped?

3. What does it mean to be "in the world, but not of the world?" Of those two phrases (in vs. of), which do you think gets the most attention in Christian circles? Are we, for example, more focused on being present in the world or remaining uninfected by the world?

4. Reflect on the Day of Pentecost in Acts 2. What significance does this have for us today? What were the results of this experience? Do we still see these results today? To what degree?

5. There are several hallmarks of Incarnational ministry listed at the end of this chapter. Write them out and talk about them. Contrast them with the "other route." What do you notice? How do you measure up? How does your church? What are the areas in which you, personally, need to do some development or some rethinking?

DAVID LEE ROTH

April 1, 1985

For millions of fans, Van Halen would no longer be the same. Sure, they would continue to tour. Sure, they would continue to make sure. Sure, they would continue to showcase Eddie's finger tapping.

But Van Halen wouldn't really be performing.

Not really, because David Lee Roth had left the band and Van Halen just wasn't the same with Sammy Hagar, never mind Mitch Malloy or Gary Cherone.

Van Halen is a little before my time, but I sympathize with these fans.
   I wouldn't be keen on U2 without Bono,
     or Coldplay without Chris Martin,
       and who could possibly fill the shoes
         of Tom Yorke or Eddie Vedder
         if they ditched Radiohead and Pearl Jam?

There is a reason they're not making Nirvana records any more.

In order for it to be Nirvana,
   it has to have Kurt Cobain,
Pearl Jam has to have Eddie Vedder,
   Radiohead, Yorke,

Coldplay is always served with Martin
        and U2 is required by law
                to make Paul Hewson put away the telethon
                and put on the shades.

Because everyone in the band has to play in order for it to be the band.

We're in a band.
        The Kingdom of Heaven is a band—
                The Body of Christ is on tour,
                and everyone is required to play.

        The Gospel must be preached to all nations.
        Mark 13.20

The mission of Jesus is to encompass all creation in his transforming presence. He came to heal the world, the whole world, not just the bits of it we see everyday. Our collective salvation will only be complete when all the world is gathered together. Only then will all of Christ's body be present.

Think about it.

If we are the Body of Christ, and God's plan is for the fullness of humanity to be (re)united in Jesus, then Jesus is currently missing bits and pieces of himself.

Christ's representation in this world will only be complete when people of every tribe, tongue, and nation come together to cooperate with God.

Because it takes all cultures and all peoples from all over the world to accurately reflect God's image.

This means we must work hard in our local churches to encourage diversity. The Church must be diverse because humanity is diverse. The Church must strive for racial, socioeconomic, political, and ethnic diversity, as well as diversity between the old and young, married and unmarried, Calvinist and Wesleyan. It is to this issue that Paul writes to the church in Ephesus:

        Christ's purpose was to create in himself one new man out of the two, thus making peace, and in this one body to reconcile both of them to God through the cross, by which he put to death their hostility...

Consequently, you are no longer foreigners and aliens, but fellow citizens with God's people and members of God's household.
Ephesians 2.15-16, 19

This letter is a celebration of Christ breaking down the walls between Jew and Gentile, between the once-seemingly irreconcilable differences that separated us from each other. Each of us are like bricks, like living stones, brought together to create a home for God.

Each of us.

That means that the true identity of the Church is not simply found in USAmerica, or Canada, or Britain, or Australia. It's not just European or African or Russian or Asian. It's all of the above, and is incomplete without all of the above.

Our motivation to see the Church broaden and include all these groups of people is two-fold:

1. The mission of Jesus is to see them all saved from sin, just as we were saved from our sin;

2. They know things about God that we don't know, and have experienced the truth of the Gospel in ways that we won't fully understand without them.

It is this second reason that drives me to write this chapter.

Most North American Christian authorities tend to think they've got a pretty strong handle on the Scriptures. They do, but they don't have a monopoly on the Scriptures. The African people have original thoughts about what the Scriptures mean in their context that don't make sense to us in North America because they have had experiences that differ strongly from our experiences.

Our recent experience has largely been of blessing;
theirs has been of sorrow, starvation, AIDS, and genocide.

Our theologies tend toward thanking God for prosperity,
seeking greater prosperity, and reminding our people to work hard because God commands us to.

Their theologies tend toward thanking God for protecting them, being at peace with God when He didn't protect loved ones who have died violently or senselessly, and asking God for strength to work even though the work they do will not bring in enough money to sustain their families.

When we bring *our* theology to Africa we tell them, in effect, that God wants them to be healthy, wealthy, and industrious.

But most of them will never see the wealth we promise, or become healthy like we're used to, or perceive any reward for their industry.

Our theology tends to be a personal, individual commitment to Jesus that no one can take away.

Theirs tends to be a community ethic in which friends and family preserve faith at home and keep each other connected.

What I'm trying to say is this: They know some stuff we don't know.

The truth is,
faith isn't just an individual encounter with Jesus; it is also a highly communal experience of belonging to the family of God.

The truth is,
hard work is given far more preeminence in Western thought than biblical thought, and the rewards we claim as a result of our work are more culturally conditioned than biblically mandated. True, the Bible instructs us to work hard and claims we will be rewarded for it; but equally true are the stories of slavery in Egypt and captivity in Assyria where hundreds of thousands of Israelites worked hard and were never rewarded for it. Hard work is no guarantee of blessing, and we forget that.

The truth is,
America has been blessed but we are not entitled to the blessings we have. The blessings we currently enjoy may not last, and we should not prescribe them to others, nor should we base our relationship with Jesus upon ensuring they do.

The truth is,
Africans know more about loving God in the midst of suffering than we do...because they've had to find out the hard way.

And we should pay attention to their thoughts about God, because, one day, we might need someone to instruct us about godly sorrow.

So back to my original point: In order for the Church to be the Church, in order for the band to be the band, it requires all of humanity to come together and represent Christ to each other.

We need the African perspective,
> the Asian perspective,
> the Mediterranean perspective,
>> to interpenetrate our American perspective
>> so we grow up in God.

This is one of the reasons why short-term missions trips are so important. When you go to another place and hear how they speak of God, you recognize your own spiritual deficiencies in areas you might not even have known existed.

I've been more challenged in my faith
> in Guatemalan dumps and African orphanages,
> in Haitian schools and Filipino cities,
> in Belizean jungles and Romanian playgrounds
>> than I ever have by sitting through an American sermon.

This chapter is about the importance of listening to people from different backgrounds teach us about their experience of God so that our own experience of God can be deepened.

QUESTIONS FOR FURTHER REFLECTION

1. Why do you think it's important for the Gospel to reach all the nations of the world? How can you help that happen? In what ways can you participate in the mission of God to heal the world?

2. What validity is there in thinking about Christian spirituality from the perspective of an African or Asian? What about if you will never travel overseas, is it still worthwhile to consider the Gospel from their perspective even if you will never share that perspective? Why? Or, why not?

PART FOUR: SOLIDARITY

WE SUFFER WITH THE ONE WHO DIED

Jesus came to live among us in our suffering. Jesus suffered on the cross. Because of the Incarnation we commit to being with one another when we suffer, and to finding courage when we suffer ourselves.

He was despised and rejected by men,
  a man of sorrows
  and familiar with suffering.

Surely he took up our infirmities
  and carried our sorrows,
      yet we considered him stricken by God,
      smitten by him and afflicted.

But he was pierced for our transgressions,
  he was crushed for our iniquities;
      the punishment that brought us peace
          was upon him
      and by his stripes we are healed.

After the suffering of his soul,
  he will see the light of life and be satisfied;
      by his knowledge my righteous servant
          will justify many
          and he will bear their iniquities.

Isaiah 53.3-5, 11

Again at Christmas did we weave
The holly round the Christmas hearth;
The silent snow possess'd the earth,
And calmly fell our Christmas-eve:

The yule-log sparkled keen with frost,
No wing of wind the region swept,
But over all things brooding slept
The quiet sense of something lost.

As in the winters left behind,
Again our ancient games had place,
The mimic picture's breathing grace,
And dance and song and hoodman-blind.

Who show'd a token of distress?
No single tear, no mark of pain:
O sorrow, then can sorrow wane?
O grief, can grief be changed to less?

O last regret, regret can die!
No--mixt with all this mystic frame,
Her deep relations are the same,
But with long use her tears are dry.

Again at Christmas did we weave
Lord Alfred Tennyson

PRETTY TV LADY

He was despised and rejected by men,
a man of sorrows
and familiar with suffering.

Surely he took up our infirmities
and carried our sorrows,
yet we considered him stricken by God,
smitten by him and afflicted.

But he was pierced for our transgressions,
he was crushed for our iniquities;
the punishment that brought us peace
was upon him
and by his stripes we are healed.

After the suffering of his soul,
he will see the light of life and be satisfied;
by his knowledge my righteous servant
will justify many
and he will bear their iniquities.

Isaiah 53.3-5, 11

Looking for Suffering?
Save on exactly what you need.
www.half.com
(Google ad-words on sidebar, after searching "suffering")

My daughter woke me up last Tuesday at 5:30am asking for potato chips. After I sent her back to bed with a cheese-stick, I found I couldn't get back to sleep and decided to watch a little television.

By some strange twist of fate I found myself watching one of the many Christian channels that I get through DirecTV. (It seems, by the way, that the number of these channels just keeps increasing, as if Christian producers took God's command to "be fruitful and multiply" to be about satellite entertainment). Usually when I find myself watching Christian TV, I know there has to be a higher purpose than my channel surfing—so I try not to be unduly critical of the content there. But that's hard.

And, preparing as I was to write this chapter on the suffering of Jesus Christ, I found it difficult not to be critical once again.

On the TV was a beautiful, thin, young, blond woman speaking passionately about God's desire to prosper His people—and that, mind you, doesn't just mean He wants you to be rich but, additionally, He also wants you to be happy and healthy and popular.

I don't want to lampoon this woman—she was, truthfully, a very good teacher and obviously loves the Lord very much—but there is another side to Christian spirituality than this.

> While it's true that God does want you to prosper (3 John 1.2), and that prosperity does, in fact, mean you will have great control over your finances, greater security in economic matters, greater resources at your disposal, and greater influence—there are no guarantees in this life that you will, in fact, prosper.

After all, many godly people have lived lives of incredible and lasting meaning without achieving all that this beautiful young lady promised on God's behalf.

Mother Theresa did not prosper,
   neither did Thomas Merton,
      Henry Nouwen,

St. Theresa of Avila,
Erasmus,
St. Augustine,
St. Clement,
                    or any of the 12 disciples.

And, while it's true that God wants you to be happy (Galatians 5.22-23; Nehemiah 8.10), there are no guarantees that life's circumstances will be conducive to happiness, only that God's Spirit will sustain you with an ever-present joy in the midst of suffering (1 Peter 1.3-9).

And while it's true that sickness is a distortion of God's plan for humanity and for Creation, there are no guarantees that we will not get sick and die.

There are no guarantees.

Not in this life.

And so I find myself wondering if those who follow Jesus because they want to be healthy, wealthy, and wise are about to encounter some pretty serious disappointment (and a pretty hefty sense of deception) when their theology comes crashing down all around them.

Like my friend Trey (not his real name), a fantastic preacher at a prosperity church that believed all the things the pretty TV lady believed—everything crashed down when Trey's wife had an affair, and then Trey lost his job through some tricky circumstances, and then the people that Trey had pastored turned against him because they felt weird now that he was a divorcee and a ministry failure. And even though Trey did nothing different, even though he could quote every Scripture about health, wealth, and wisdom in both Testaments (backwards, no less), Trey's God failed him.

Because Trey's God didn't work the way He was supposed to.

Now, I don't write all of this to depress you. If your one hope in this world is that somehow God will reverse your current, miserable, circumstances, please don't feel like I just pulled the rug out from under you.

Jesus can, and does, work to help us in real life.

But the process is slower than most pretty TV people make it out to be, and the goal is more holistic.

To understand Jesus—which will then help us to understand God and His plan for each of us to be (re)formed into His image, the image of Christ—we must look to the Scriptures. And, in order to correctly interpret the Second Testament Scriptures we must look at the First Testament Scriptures which serve as the control group for our conclusions.

> The Old Testament is the thing that keeps us from making up whatever nonsense we choose about Jesus.
> **N.T. Wright**

In the First Testament there is a character called the Servant, spoken of chiefly in Isaiah 40-66 (we touched on this in second two, KENOSIS). This Servant was one who would suffer on behalf of God's people, thereby protecting them from any suffering they might bring upon themselves.

Jesus is that Servant.

> When evening came, many who were demon-possessed were brought to him, and he drove out the spirits with a word and healed all the sick. This was to fulfill what was spoken through the prophet Isaiah: *He took up our infirmities and carried our diseases.*
> **Matthew 8.16-17**

> He himself bore our sins in his body on the tree, so that we might die to sins and live for righteousness; by his wounds you have been healed.
> **1 Peter 2.24**

Jesus suffered on behalf of sinful humanity and through his atoning death on the cross we have unprecedented access to God.

But, for our intents and purposes here, the part I want you to pay attention to is found in those first two words: Jesus suffered.

The picture we see of God, given to us by Jesus on the cross, is that of a deserted, bruised, bleeding, and dying deity. His death lends new meaning to human suffering, and new dignity to those who suffer, because he did it too. Our God knows what it's like to suffer, and though our present experiences in this life often hurt and scar us beyond what we think we could possibly ever endure, it is the image of God-on-a-stick that buoys us with hope and leads us into the future.

Jesus' whole entire life was one continual Passion, a third-of-a-century-long martyrdom. He was born a martyr, lying in a straw bed with the hay pricking his infant skin; He died a martyr, on Golgotha, for crimes he did not commit. Christmas and Easter are twin holidays because they both celebrate the suffering of God, the lamb who takes away the sin of the world.

Jesus came to suffer and die for sinful humanity. That's why he came. That's how he died. His suffering was proof of his love, and it is precisely that love that compels me to love him.

Which brings us back full circle.

If we align ourselves with Jesus, let us ensure that we are giving our allegiance to the proper God.

> The Incarnate God,
>> revealed in both Testaments in Scripture,
>> does not come to us promising health,
>>> wealth,
>>> and wisdom.

> He comes to us, in pain, and he suffers.

> He dies, for us,
>> and promises that the same suffering he endured
>> we, too, will endure for his sake.

> He felt God's absence,
>> like we, too, will feel the absence of God.

> But then he rose from the dead,
>> coming out of the grave into new life on the other side
>> and we, too, have inherited
>>> that promise of new life
>>> and can begin living it now.

To set the record straight: *That's* what it means to prosper even as your soul prospers.

In the end, I am wealthier than I would be apart from the guidance of Christ. I am happier, more full of a resident joy, than I would be without the Spirit alive and at work in me. I am healthier because of the wisdom of godly people who counsel me to exercise and eat right, and I listen to them because the Spirit instructs me to pay attention to their wisdom instead of my proclivity for sloth and gluttony.

But the reason I am healthier, wealthier, and wiser is not because that's what Christ promised and delivered. It's because I know the One who died for me, and I know what he endured, and I know that his Spirit and power are working in me, each moment, to grow me up into a bigger person.

The net result of faithfulness and connection to God is an internal fire that fuels my life toward good things.

I don't hold on to Jesus in order to get those things, I get those things as a by-product of cooperating with God and healing the world.

QUESTIONS FOR FURTHER REFLECTION

1. Contrast the popular message of the "prosperity Gospel" (the message of the pretty lady on TV) with the message of the Servant. What are the main differences? Why do you think the prosperity message is so popular these days? Though it does provide hope, what are some of the dangers involved with promising prosperity?

2. Take a moment and consider how much Jesus endured on the cross. This chapter doesn't go into the gory details, but some understanding can be gleaned by reading John chapter 19. Read that chapter now. How does it affect you?

3. Having read the entire chapter, take a moment and consider prosperity as it's defined at the end. How is this different than the message of the TV lady? Which of these two messages makes for a better way to live? Which makes a better infomercial? Which of these two messages will lead you deeper into a relationship with Jesus Christ, and why?

WHEN YOUR JEEP GETS STUCK

The first time I went off-roading was with my friend Vince, four days after buying my brand new 2004 Jeep Wrangler TJ. Within the first hour, we found ourselves with only two wheels grounded—front left, rear right—as we teetered above a steep incline. One wrong move would've meant rolling the Jeep, totaling it, or worse.

I panicked.

I remember hyper-ventilating, my only thoughts weighing whether or not I could abandon the Jeep and talk to my insurance agent before having to tell Carmel, or whether it would just be simpler to die then and there.

Vince, thankfully, did not panic.

Having been in similarly sticky situations many, many times (including losing his Jeep in the middle of a river and saved from going over a waterfall by a divinely placed rock caught on it's skid plate), Vince knew what to do.

But he made me do it.

It was my Jeep, after all.

Slowly, we turned the wheels to face downhill and Vince leaned out of the passenger door, putting all his weight on the front left tire. There was a moment of doubt when it seemed like we'd roll, until, giving it a little gas, we made it.

I have Vince to thank for that. Had it not been for him, I'd have either rolled the Jeep or just left it there and sorted the mess out with Carmel later on (I confess, making up a story about auto-theft seemed like a good option).

Vince had been through stuff like that, so he could coach me when it was my Jeep on the line.

All Christians have a Vince in Christ Jesus; or, rather, Vince is like Jesus—there when you need him, calming you down, talking you down, telling you it's gonna be okay, that he's been here before and isn't going to abandon you.

Jesus suffered and died, and so we take strength from him when we find ourselves hurt, alone, scared, anxious, grieving, wounded, doubtful, compromised, accused, hated, and in despair.

> God is the great companion – the fellow sufferer who understands.
> **Alfred North Whitehead**

Truthfully, I have been spared much suffering in my life. It's important for me to acknowledge that, especially given many who read this will have endured far more pain, more embarrassment, more sickness, and more loss than me. I am no expert on suffering, having had little first hand experience, but I have seen others take remarkable strength from Jesus in the middle of some extraordinarily bad circumstances.

I have seen people with no hope, and no help, summon the courage to keep going because of Jesus.

I have seen people with nothing to live for, with every bridge burned and every relationship spoiled, keep living and turning their lives around because of Jesus.

One of the great privileges of pastoring is seeing people take strength and comfort in Jesus.

> It makes all the difference to know there's someone else screaming alongside you—and that's the point of the Incarnation. I can see that

so clearly now. God came into the world and screamed alongside us. Interesting idea, that.

Susan Howatch, via Rob Bell's *Drops like Stars*

And Jesus did suffer.

In his book, *Vintage Jesus*, Mark Driscoll compiles a list of Jesus' hard times:

- ☐ Jesus was tempted by the Devil himself (Matthew 4.1-10).
- ☐ Jesus had money troubles that included being poor (2 Corinthians 8.9), getting ripped off (John 12.6), struggling to pay his taxes (Matthew 17.27), and being homeless (Matthew 8.20).
- ☐ People attacked Jesus by spreading vicious rumors (Matthew 26.57-60), physically abusing him (Matthew 26.67-68), and mocking and spitting on him (Matthew 27.27-31).
- ☐ Jesus was continually jacked with by religious neatniks (Matthew 9.11, 34; 12.2, 14, 38; 16.1).
- ☐ Jesus had some bummer days marked by loneliness (Mark 14.32-34; 15.34), deep sorrow (Matthew 26.37), exhaustion (Matthew 8.24), and weeping (Luke 19.41; John 11.35).
- ☐ Jesus' friends were a joke and no help in times of crisis (Matthew 26.36-46)—they turned their backs on him (Matthew 26.69-75) and betrayed him (Matthew 26.47-50).
- ☐ Jesus' family thought he was a nut job (Mark 3.21; John 7.5).
- ☐ Jesus turned to God the Father but did not have all his prayers answered as he requested (Matthew 26.42).
- ☐ Jesus bled (Luke 22.44; John 19.34).
- ☐ Jesus died (Luke 23.46).
- ☐ Jesus used his last breath to forgive those who destroyed him (Luke 23.34).

When you've been dumped,
    fired,
    divorced,
    bereaved,
    stilted,
    jeered
        and find yourself generally miserable,
          you can take strength in Jesus.

        He knows what you're going through.

He had dark, dark days
and his only guarantee
was that the salvation he would bring
would come *after* he died.

Without knowing all this about the earthly life of Jesus, we'd have no confidence in turning to him when our lives stink. We'd make the mistake—as many belligerently still do—of thinking that he spent most of his time telling stories to kids and petting lambs.

But no, Jesus acts as our partner when we suffer as one who has previously endured what we must now endure, and he sits with us providing strength and comfort. That doesn't diminish our pain, but it does validate it. It lets us know that our suffering, though real, is shared suffering.

Because Jesus suffered the severity of being human.

Lo – I am with you always, even to the very end of the age.
Matthew 28.20

QUESTIONS FOR FURTHER REFLECTION

1. Have you ever had an experience in which you found yourself in trouble and were glad for the company of a calm, experienced friend? Share your story with some friends, perhaps those in your Satellite group. How did you feel?

2. Can you think of a difficult time when you looked to Jesus for strength? Did he help? If so, how? If he didn't help, take a moment and describe your disappointment. What do you wish would have happened? What help were you looking for?

3. Take a moment and review the Scripture references and bullet points provided by Mark Driscoll concerning Jesus' hard times. How many of these do you relate with personally? In what ways?

A PERSON IS A PERSON
THROUGH OTHER PERSONS

When people die, it's important to be there for the ones left behind. It's not necessarily important to say the right things, or somehow to be spiritual, or do a bunch of stuff. What's important, is just being there.

Holding them together.

I've been with a mother in Port-au-Prince who had just lost her newborn,
and with a daughter in Johannesburg who had just lost her mother,
and with a husband in Surrey who had just lost his wife.

I've been in far too many situations like these, and I've never felt smart, or well-prepared, or wise in any of them.

But I was there, and in the end, it was being there that counted.

Bearing witness to their pain, counts.

Not leaving them,
like their dearly departed have left, counts –
even if my staying is only temporary
...for as long as I'm not leaving, it counts.

Holding them physically, counts.

These things count because they tell hurting people that they aren't alone. We are sharing something together, even if they are sharing more of it than I am.

Death is not the only occasion for solidarity, for us to lock arms with others, for togetherness, for community.

When others suffer, it's important for us to be with them bearing witness, staying, holding.

Christ does that for us, through his Holy Spirit, our comforter.

> I will ask the Father, and he will give you another Comforter to be with you forever—the Spirit of truth.
> **John 14.16-17a**

One of those most frequently noted attributes of Jesus is compassion. For example:

- [ ] Jesus was moved by compassion to heal (Mark 1.41; Luke 7.13; Matthew 20.34).
- [ ] Jesus had compassion on the crowd(s) (Matthew 9.36, 14.14, 15.32; Mark 6.34, 8.2).
- [ ] Jesus used compassion in his stories of the prodigal son (Luke 15), the Good Samaritan (Luke 10), and the king who forgives debts (Matthew 18).

Far from the popular cinematic portrayals of Jesus as a wan, expressionless, and holy drone (Mel Gibson's *The Passion of the Christ* aside), the Jesus we see in the Bible is deeply emotional, empathetic, and motivated to action by virtue of his shared sense of humanity with others.

It is this shared sense of humanity, which the Africans call *ubuntu*, which lies at the very heart of shadowing God and being present with others in the midst of their pain. The more we are filled with God's Spirit, the more committed we become to hospitality, to solidarity, to compassion—the more human we become.

> A person is a person through other persons.
> **Traditional African saying**

We don't come fully formed into this world—we come as infants, as beginners, as the impressionable young looking to be imprinted with our humanity. We learn how to walk, how to think, how to act and behave and love from other people. We need other people. Other people need us. We need each other to be human, for we were made for togetherness, family, community, fellowship, and love.

That's why it's so important to be with others when they suffer—to remind them that we share something. We share our humanity. Knowing that simple, basic truth can powerful, and that it can sustain our dignity in the midst of humiliation, our courage in the face of tragedy, or our integrity in the face of persecution.

Every person is a human being, and we demonstrate the truth of God's image in us when we reach out to each other in love and comfort.

> We have to think of every human being, even the oddest, most villainous or miserable, as one to whom Jesus Christ is Brother and God is Father; and we have to deal with him on this assumption.
> **Karl Barth**
>
> [Christ] had a face like every one's, a face like all men's faces...I thought 'what sort of Christ is this?'...suddenly my heart sank, and I came to myself. Only then did I realize that just such a face – a face like all men's faces – is the face of Christ.
> **Ivan Turgenev, 19thC Russian novelist**

I have a friend who used to be depressed all time. She was cool, smart, funny, and had lots going for her, but she was always bummed out. My friend Deb spent a fair amount of time with Kari (not her name) just being present with her, but that never seemed to wholly work. Kari always seemed to slip back into a funky mood.

One day, Kari made a change. She decided she wasn't going to be so focused on her own mood or her own problems, but that she would devote her life instead to helping the homeless. She volunteered at a place called the Union Gospel Mission in downtown Vancouver and began serving meals three times a week to people living in cardboard homes and driving shopping carts.

Kari's love for Jesus lead her to believe that life wasn't all about her, even when she was feeling upset. She began to understand that there were others who required her presence, much in the same way that she'd often required Deb's presence.

Her life changed.

Like any of us, Kari still gets bummed out about life and still turns to her friends for help, but she values that help more now. She knows the difference that just being there can make in the lives of other people, and she's not just a recipient of care now, but a courier as well.

> There is an essential unity between contemplation and action, between prayer and politics, between spirituality and justice...spirituality is justice. My involvement flows, I hope, from my religion.
> **Desmond Tutu**

This is one of the reasons I think it's important for every church to be involved in helping others, both locally and internationally. Even if all our efforts barely amount to anything in the grand scheme of things—even if the food we provide to an orphanage doesn't solve world hunger, or the love we give to indigenous pastors leading rural churches in India doesn't cover their annual budget—it does make a difference.

To us, just as much as to them.

> Jesus stands at the door and knocks, in complete reality. He asks you for help in the form of a beggar, in the form of a ruined human being in torn clothing. He confronts you in every person that you meet. Christ walks on the earth as your neighbor as long as there are people. He walks on the earth as the one through whom God calls you, speaks to you, and makes his demands.
> **Dietrich Bonhoeffer**

QUESTIONS FOR FURTHER REFLECTION

1. Have you ever been with someone after they've lost a loved one? Describe how they felt. Describe how you felt. What have they told you about those times when you were with them after their loss? How meaningful was it for them that you were there? Has anyone ever been there for you?

2. What do you think about this idea that "a person is a person through other persons?" Does this make sense to you? In what way? How dependant do you think we really are on each other? How dependant do you think we really are on God? What's the difference?

3. What do you think happens to us when we make a commitment to be with others in their time of need?

4. What can we do to help others in need in other parts of the world? How can we use our privileges to benefit those in the Sudan, or in Bosnia, or in Haiti?

BIG BOY PANTS

Nobody said it would be easy.

Following the way of Jesus is hard—it requires sacrifice, endurance, constant commitment to staying fueled by the Spirit, and a constant decision to not rely on our own strength.

The way of Jesus involves taking up our cross, every day, and following him into pain, into hardship, sometimes even into conflict or loss of life. We forget that, sometimes. Our thoughts tend towards the benefits of serving Jesus. But we forget that there was a crucifixion before there ever was a resurrection.

> If anyone would come after me, he must deny himself and take up his cross and follow me. For whoever wants to save his life will lose it, but whoever loses his life for me and for the gospel will save it.
> **Mark 8.34-35**

And yet, so many of us flounder and give up at the slightest bit of resistance. Never mind taking up our cross, most of the time we can barely manage taking time to pray.

Over the years, I think I've heard every possible excuse ever invented for why Christian spirituality is too much work. All of these things seem reasonable at the outset, but given what we know to be true, both about the sacrifice Jesus made and the cost he forewarned us we would pay for following him, they quickly start feeling pretty flimsy.

> It's hard to pray,
>> I don't know what to say or what I'm allowed to ask for.

> It's hard to read my Bible,
>> because the language is sometimes difficult to understand and I usually only have time before I go to bed and then I feel bad reading it because I know I'll fall asleep.

> It's hard to serve at the church,
>> we're just so busy that giving our time to the church feels like one more thing we have to do, and we're pulled in too many directions as it is.

> It's hard to give generously and sacrificially of our money,
>> we're barely making it as it is and God understands that there are others who could give more and have it cost less...plus, our money doesn't make a difference anyway.

> It's hard to get into meaningful relationships with other Christians,
>> especially "mature" Christians because they know so much and I feel so stupid when I ask about stuff.

> It's hard to serve in the community,
>> because I don't know which places I can trust to be run well and I'm not sure I'm making a difference anyway.

Sure. All that stuff is hard. But even if we did all that hard stuff, it still wouldn't really qualify as "taking up our cross", would it? I mean, Jesus wasn't referring to the cross as a metaphor—he actually picked up a cross and then got pinned to it, like he was part of Caesar's butterfly collection.

> To be incarnate is to be crucified.
> **Andrew Root**

I don't want to belittle anyone's personal pain. I do, however, want to point out that our idea of what "suffering for Jesus" is sucks.

When it's too hard to read the Scriptures, too tough to pray, and too much to ask to give money or serve or get into accountability with another believer, then you're not willing to suffer. Not even a bit.

And that realization should hurt.

In fact, I'm writing it, with the full support of Scripture, to hurt you. To sting. I don't want you to feel guilty—God wants you to change.

Begin at the beginning with the basics: prayer, study, fellowship, service, financial sacrifice, generosity. That way, you'll be ready for the intermediate stuff of faith.

> Like newborn babies, crave pure spiritual milk, so that by it you may grow up in your salvation, now that you have tasted that the Lord is good.
> **1 Peter 2.2-3**
>
> Brothers, I could not address you as spiritual but as worldly—mere infants in Christ. I gave you milk, not solid food, for you were not yet ready for it. Indeed, you are still not ready. You are still worldly. For since there is jealousy and quarreling among you...
> **1 Corinthians 3.1-3**

It's time for each of us to put on our spiritual big boy pants. It's time for us to stop making excuses, to make a firm commitment in our hearts, and begin living the life God has intended for us.

And, yes, that life will be hard sometimes, but it will also be worth it.

> Dear friends, do not be surprised at the painful trial you are suffering, as though something strange were happening to you. But rejoice that you participate in the sufferings of Christ, so that you may be overjoyed when his glory is revealed.
> **1 Peter 4.12-13**
>
> Enter through the narrow gate. For wide is the gate and broad is the road that leads to destruction, and many enter through it. But small is the gate and narrow the road that leads to life, and only a few find it.
> **Matthew 7.13-14**

QUESTIONS FOR FURTHER REFLECTION

1. What kinds of suffering should we expect to face in this life? What about suffering particularly related to our Christian commitments? Have you ever experienced any persecution, mockery, or hatred because of your faith? How did you handle that?

2. Of the excuses that are listed in this chapter for not prayer, or reading the Bible, etc. which ones most sound like you? What will you do to get past those excuses? Who do you know that can help you?

3. Perhaps the most important realization in the process of Christian maturity is that we cannot grow up spiritually on our own. We need the Spirit to work in and through us. What can you do to ensure that the Holy Spirit stays entrusted with your development?

PART FIVE: CONFESSION

WE WORSHIP THE ONE WHO SAVES

Jesus Christ, both fully God and man, came into the world to a redeem lost humanity and restore a ruined creation. Because of the Incarnation, we worship God.

Beyond all question, the mystery of godliness is great:

> [Christ] appeared in a body,
> > was vindicated by the Spirit,
> > was seen by angels,
> > was preached among the nations,
> > was believed on in the world,
> > was taken up in glory.

1 Timothy 3.16

FROM THE WORD

FROM THE WORLD

Turning and turning in the widening gyre
The falcon cannot hear the falconer;
Things fall apart; the centre cannot hold;
Mere anarchy is loosed upon the world,
The blood-dimmed tide is loosed, and everywhere
The ceremony of innocence is drowned;
The best lack all conviction, while the worst
Are full of passionate intensity.
Surely some revelation is at hand;
Surely the Second Coming is at hand.
The Second Coming! Hardly are those words out
When a vast image out of Spritus Mundi
Troubles my sight: somewhere in the sands of the desert
A shape with lion body and the head of a man,
A gaze blank and pitiless as the sun,
Is moving its slow thighs, while all about it
Reel shadows of the indignant desert birds.
The darkness drops again; but now I know
That twenty centuries of stony sleep
were vexed to nightmare by a rocking cradle,
And what rough beast, its hour come round at last,
Slouches towards Bethlehem to be born?

The Second Coming
William Butler Yeates

NOT PEACE BUT A SWORD

In the beginning was the Word, and the Word was with God, and the Word was God. He was with God in the beginning. Through him all things were made; without him nothing was made that has been made. In him was life, and that life was the light of men. The light shines in the darkness, but the darkness has not understood it.

There came a man who was sent from God; his name was John. He came as a witness to testify concerning that light, so that through him all men might believe. He himself was not the light; he came only as a witness to the light. The true light that gives light to every man was coming into the world.

He was in the world, and though the world was made through him, the world did not recognize him. He came to that which was his own, but his own did not receive him. Yet to all who received him, to those who believed in his name, he gave the right to become children of God— children born not of natural descent, nor of human decision or a husband's will, but born of God.

The Word became flesh and made his dwelling among us. We have seen his glory, the glory of the One and Only, who came from the Father, full of grace and truth.

John testifies concerning him. He cries out, saying, "This was he of

whom I said, 'He who comes after me has surpassed me because he was before me.'" From the fullness of his grace we have all received one blessing after another. For the law was given through Moses; grace and truth came through Jesus Christ. No one has ever seen God, but God the One and Only, who is at the Father's side, has made him known.
John 1.1-18

This chapter is about the fact that Jesus is God, a proposition that rightly startles most people when they are confronted by it. Most of my friends, for example, feel pretty comfortable with the idea that Jesus was a great moral teacher, or the noble and virtuous founder of (what was supposed to be) a new religion based on faith, hope, and love. But they're not crazy about Jesus being one-and-the-same with God, and they're really not convinced he saw himself that way either.

Come off it, alright?

> Once Christianity affirms that a man is at the same time God, it stands alone in the world.
> **Leonardo Boff**

Well, in order to show that the Christian belief in Jesus' divinity is justified we have to start with Jesus' claims about himself. Did he, or did he not, claim to be God?

Turns out, according to the four credible biographies we have of Jesus, that he did (we have, by the way, many dozens of additional biographies about Jesus, but they are largely unreliable and contradictory. Furthermore, when—like the Gospel of Thomas or the Gospel of Peter—they differ in their estimation of Jesus from the canonical Gospels of Matthew, Mark, Luke, and John, it is to diminish Jesus' humanity, not his divinity).

- He claimed to be the same, to be One, with God (John 8.57-59, 10.30-33, 12.44-46, 14.6-9).
- He claimed authority to forgive sins, something only God could do, and was accused of blasphemy because of it (Mark 2.1-12).
- He accepted worship from his disciples, worship that reserved for God (Matthew 9.18, 14.32-33, 15.25, 28.9, 28.17).

Based on these (and many other) claims, famed author C.S. Lewis noted that there are really only three credible options for people when confronted with Jesus:

> Either he made claims to divinity that were false and he knew
>   it, making him a madman;
> or he made claims to divinity that were false and he didn't
>   know it, making him on par with a nutjob who claims to be a
>   poached egg;
> or he made claims to divinity that were true, in which case he
>   must be God and must be worshipped.

The three choices, popularly reconceived, are that Jesus was either bad, mad, or God.

A lot of people aren't crazy about Lewis' trilemma, noting that it limits all possibilities down to just three. Some, for example, think there may be a fourth option—that maybe the biographies containing Jesus' claims are historically inaccurate or fanciful reconstructions of his life and teachings, in which case the whole Jesus thing could just be a Legend.

But there is simply too much evidence supporting the historicity of the Gospels for this last opinion to be tenable.

In short, the Gospel accounts are trustworthy, and Jesus did claim to be God, so we're left with either a Lunatic, a Liar, or the Lord.

The Christian faith is based on the last of these options: that Jesus Christ really was and is God of All, Creator of the Universe, and Second Person of the Holy Trinity.

Much of our basis for this belief is rooted in the prologue to John's Gospel, which begins with the same words as Genesis:

In the beginning was the Word...

That's not an accident. John is talking about both original creation and about God's project of (re)creation, both of which are accomplished through His Word.

In the First Testament, God regularly acts by means of His Word (Genesis 1-2, 33.6), and His Word is the one thing that will outlast all creation (Isaiah 40.6-8), even after the Word brings life, healing, and restoration into it (Isaiah 55.10-11).

The Word was there at the very beginning, and now the Word is here again in a new way. Just as the Word interrupted the darkness in Genesis 1, so now the Word comes to interrupt darkness in John 1.

As John makes clear, Jesus Christ is the Word made flesh, which means that Jesus Christ was present and active at the time of the original creation. He made the world, and now he's come to save the world.

Problem is, nobody recognizes him.

We have the same problem now—we recognize the wisdom and importance of Jesus, but we miss the fact that he's the Word, he's God, and when we worship Jesus we're worshipping God.

What's more, all worship of God must now go through Jesus.

This is why Christianity causes such tension and division among friends and families—because by virtue of our faith in Jesus, we're very narrow-minded about spirituality.

> Do not suppose that I have come to bring peace to the earth.
> I did not come to bring peace,
> but a sword.
> For I have come to turn a man against his father,
> a daughter against her mother,
> a daughter-in-law against her mother-in-law -
>
> a man's enemies
> will be the members of his own household.
> **Matthew 10.24-36**

Every time we make an assertion about Christianity, in order to be faithful to Jesus Christ, we are forced to make an accusation about every other belief system. We are, in effect, always calling the leaders and holy men of other religions into question because Christianity suffers no competition.

You simply cannot buy into the person of Jesus and, simultaneously, the claims of Buddha, Mohammed, or the Bhagavad Gita.

> Jesus Christ is still alive and he embodies his teachings. It is a profound mistake, therefore, to treat Christ as simply the founder of a set of

moral, ethical, or social teaching. The Lord Jesus and his teaching are one. The Medium and the Message are One. Christ is the incarnation of the Kingdom of God and the Sermon on the Mount.
Len Sweet and Frank Viola

Christianity is unique among the world's religions because of its outrageous claims concerning Jesus Christ. Jesus, alone among the leaders of all religion and philosophy, cannot be separated from his teachings. Buddha, Socrates, Confucius, Mohammed, and Moses all instruct their followers to obey their teachings. Jesus, in contrast, says: *follow me.*

Follow me.
Matthew 8.22b

This, in the end, is why it's important for us to constantly confess that the One we worship is the One who saves.

We worship Jesus Christ, Second Person of the Trinity and very-God Himself, because he descended to earth to live among us, die for us, and resurrect ahead of us.

QUESTIONS FOR FURTHER REFLECTION

1. Have you ever had anyone express disbelief about the divinity of Jesus? Have you ever felt doubtful of this? What convinced you? Or, if you remain unconvinced, what kind of proof would you require?

2. Review Lewis' trilemma (the Lunatic, Liar, Lord argument rehearsed at the beginning of the chapter). How compelling do you find this argument? Had you ever heard it before? What kind of person do you think would be convinced by this line of reasoning?

3. Take a few moments and read John 1.1-14. Make a list of all the things the Word has done, as recorded in this passage. What do you notice about the Word? How is this different than what you'd previously thought about God? In what ways is it the same?

4. Have you ever experience tension or conflict because of your faith in Jesus Christ? How did you resolve it? If you could re-live those moments, what would you have done differently in order to better represent Jesus in that situation?

THE POWER PEW

It didn't take long after Jesus ascended to heaven for people to begin speculating about who he was and what he did (and, later on, they also began to wonder about what he was and who he did, resulting in some of the wilder speculations courtesy of Dan Brown and *The DaVinci Code*).

The early church was governed by apostolic letters and Jesus' biographies that they considered both useful and authoritative. These texts were collected, screened, and checked for credibility against eye witnesses of Jesus' life including his mother, his brothers, and his earliest followers.

But there were other thoughts about Jesus that didn't check out with those sources. Some of these, more fanciful, theories imagined Jesus to be something other than God Incarnate. They thought of Jesus as a kind of magic man, or God, sure, but God uninfected by the human condition.

They imagined God was too holy and too pure to be contaminated by real humanity, so the humanity of Jesus was really just a sham, like a great Halloween outfit or a thermal shell.

This, by the way, is the major difference between the Christian doctrine of the Incarnation and incarnation as it's celebrated in other religions.

In the cult of Egypt, for example, the god Osiris sometimes incarnates himself as wheat before the harvest and the god Ra incarnates himself as the sun during the day—but those are just metaphors, not actual incarnations.

In Hinduism, Vishnu sometimes takes on human form, but never for an entire lifetime. Vishnu only pulls out the human-suit when it suits his purpose.

In Buddhism, finally, incarnation is seen as a repeatable failure until final success—as if life's a video game where you keep on dying and dying and dying until you pass the level and win the online trophy. If anything, the part where people are incarnated in Buddhism is a failure, not—like Christ's Incarnation—the medium for salvation, *kenosis*, mission, solidarity, and confession.

The real problem with the Gnostics was that they felt that everything about this world was a waste and that the only real value in anything was spiritual value. Consequently, if something wasn't spiritual enough for them—if it was too concerned with work, the daily business of running a house, nutrition, play, etc.—then it was absolutely ungodly.

But this, of course, is the exact opposite message to that of Jesus. Jesus came and lived among us, ratifying basic human affairs and existence. He didn't tell us that normal humanity was a waste, he showed us that normal humanity was brilliantly godly when fired by the Spirit.

Again, Mark Driscoll provides a helpful summary of the normality of Jesus' life in his book *Vintage Jesus*. Inside he notes that Jesus:

- was born of a woman (Galatians 4.4).
- had a normal body of flesh and bones (Luke 24.39).
- grew up as a boy (Luke 2.52).
- had a family (Luke 4.16).
- obeyed his parents (Luke 2.51).
- worshipped God (Luke 4.16) and prayed (Mark 1.35, 6.46).
- worked as a carpenter (Mark 6.3).
- got hungry (Matthew 4.2) and thirsty (John 4.7).
- asked for information (Mark 9.16-21).
- was stressed (John 31.21).
- was astonished (Mark 6.6; Luke 7.9).
- was happy (Luke 10.21-24; John 15.11, 17.13; Hebrews 12.2,22).
- told jokes (Matthew 7.6, 23.24; Mark 4.21).
- had compassion (Mark 1.41; Luke 7.13).
- had male and female friends he loved (John 11.3-5).

- ☐ gave encouraging compliments (Mark 12.41-44).
- ☐ loved children (Matthew 19.13-15).
- ☐ celebrated holidays (Luke 2.41).
- ☐ went to parties (Matthew 11.19).
- ☐ loved his mom (John 19.26-27).

I think this Gnostic-thing is still a problem today. Too many Christians want everything to be super-spiritual at the expense of being human.

For example, when I was growing up we had a gaggle of Christian keeners we called "the power pew." The Power Pew, comprised of three couples, never thought we prayed enough, thought we laughed too much and disgraced ourselves because of our mirth, never thought we quoted enough Bible verses, thought we went to too many movies and enjoyed too much secular music, never thought we fasted enough, thought we spent too much time having friends over for dinner without witnessing to them, and so on.

They just never believed that anybody else was spiritual enough to be called Christian.

That was fifteen years ago.

Today, all three couples are divorced and have one or both ex-spouses with some addiction. None attend church, let alone serve, and none consider themselves spiritual like they once were.

Such marital disasters are complex and cannot be reduced to just one explanation;
however,
> I strongly suspect
>> that any marriage in which laughter is frowned upon,
>> in which meals should only be for nourishment,
>> in which sex should only be for procreation,
>> in which music should only be for psalmistry,
>> in which friendship should only be evangelistic,
>> in which literature should only be doctrinal,
>>> will self-destruct eventually.

Because it's not a marriage between two people, it's a marriage between two people trying very, very hard not to actually be people.

Everything that Jesus validated in his earthly life, the Gnostics (and the Power

Pew) have tried to invalidate by being holier than him, as if Jesus had merely pointed us in the direction of holiness hoping that we could somehow improve upon his sinlessness.

We must understand that God's glory was seen through the humanity of Jesus, not his deity. It's not the miracles of Jesus that are unique—deities of all stripes have claimed miraculous powers for millennia—but the ordinary, everyday-ness of Jesus' love and friendship, family and finance.

God's glory is seen through Jesus' normality, but it is seen with a certain hiddenness. Like peering into a side view mirror while driving, Jesus' humanity reminds us that God is closer than the object in the mirror appears.

Which means that God is closer to us than we might think, too; because we don't have to be divine in order for God to love us. In fact, the only prerequisite for God's love is that we are human.

> We may want the spiritual without the fleshly; we may want the cosmic without the concrete. But if the Word is ever to be loved and shared, we must risk embodiment, which is always concrete and ordinary. There God is both perfectly hidden and perfectly revealed.
> **G.K. Chesterton**

The one thing we've all got to understand here is that God is Christ-like. Jesus is like an authorized visual aid to understanding God. He, and he alone in his humanity, is capable of disclosing God to us.

> He can show us God, because he is God;
> > He can show God to us, because he is human.

If we limit Christ by making him all God and not human,
> then he is incapable of identifying with us and his atoning sacrifice doesn't actually atone for anything because it doesn't fit.

> Sinful humanity required a perfect human sacrifice to atone for our sins.
> > If Jesus wasn't human-enough, then his death would have been the metaphysical equivalent of trying to stick scrap metal into a pop machine in hopes of fooling the weights inside.

We only get Pepsi if Jesus was human.

If we limit Christ by making him all human and not God,

> then he is incapable of saving us and his atoning sacrifice was just a largely-ignored martyrdom, one of many in the Roman Empire.

> Sinful humanity required God to get involved in our condition and deal with

> > our sin. If Jesus wasn't divine-enough, then his death would have been the metaphysical equivalent of the naked guy running across center field at a Detroit Lions game, thinking he's one of the players but really only playing the fool.

We only score if Jesus was God.

> In non-theological terms, Christians must learn to live stereoscopically, with bi-focal vision: to hold two opposite things together, not blending them or conflating them or reconciling them but bringing them together until they symphonize at a higher level.
> **Len Sweet**

This book is about the fact that Jesus was both fully God and fully man. This chapter has been about the latter.

Jesus was a dude.

> Get over it.

QUESTIONS FOR FURTHER REFLECTION

1. Have you ever been confronted with the speculative theories concerning Jesus (like, for example, that he moved to America, or married Mary Magdalene, etc)? What was your first reaction? How did you respond? What did you do to try and discover whether or not these theories were true or just highly imaginative? What did you find out?

2. Have you ever been confronted with the theory that the Incarnation of Jesus Christ was just a re-working of other ancient myths (like, for example, the cult of the Caesars, or the story of Osiris, etc)? What was your first reaction? How did you respond? What did you do to try and discover whether or not these theories were true or just highly imaginative? What did you find out?

3. Do you know anyone who's "too heavenly minded to be of any earthly good?" How do they make you feel? Do you think Jesus would make you feel this way? What do you think Jesus would say to a person who seems to hate this life, this world, and everything associated with it?

NEIGHBORS, CONVICTS, PETS

You are my friends if you do what I command. I no longer call you servants, because a servant does not know his master's business. Instead, I have called you friends, for everything that I learned from my Father I have made known to you. You did not choose me, but I chose you and appointed you to go and bear fruit—fruit that will last. Then the Father will give you whatever you ask in my name. This is my command: Love each other.
John 15.14-17

One of the most frequent terms used in the Second Testament to refer to Christians is "dear friends" (1 Corinthians 10.14; Philippians 2.12, 4.1; Hebrews 6.9; 1 Peter 2.11, 4.12; and many others). Friendship, clearly, has spiritual significance and never more so than in our relationship with Jesus Christ.

When Jesus was alive he had friends: the disciples (especially Peter, James, and John), the collection of female followers known as "the women", his mother—and now that he lives again he has some new friends—you and me.

No longer do I call you servants...but friends.
John 15.15

It means something to be called the friend of God.

Most of us, though, don't think of ourselves as Jesus' friends (let alone God's, when we make that distinction).

> We typically think of ourselves as something like polite, but distant,
>> neighbors who see each other from time to time but have
>> nothing in common and nothing to talk about;
> or we think of ourselves as escaped convicts,
>> on the run from God's flashlight and Doberman Pinschers
>> while the angels in the SS track us through life;
> or at best we think of ourselves as pets, faithfully staying next to God
>> in hopes that He will dole out more treats than torment.

Perhaps, on a cognitive level, we'd scoff at each of these descriptions. We know they aren't really true. But, strangely, we act as if they are true. We are dismissive of God—not aware of our inability to fully know Him, but unconcerned that we might know more of Him if we cared to—and we are scared of God—not the holy fear of Isaiah, but frightful terror—and we buddy up to God—not in love, but out of a desire to be blessed.

A major reason we're stuck as neighbors, convicts, or pets is that we simply cannot get our heads around friendship.

And the reason we cannot get our head around friendship goes back to the central theme of this book: Jesus came to live here, with us.

God with us.

God, our ally, our support, our comfort, our friend.

It's important to know that this is the God we worship, our friend-God, because you
become like what you worship. The kind of God we worship is one who makes friends with those lower than Himself.

We are wired for worship, there is something within us that calls out to the beyond, but we are also fallen and sinful. It is our sin that leads us away from worshipping God, and it is our sin that leads us to create other things to worship. Sadly, we often create things to worship that are of lesser worth than we are and that create a disdain for others (sometimes we are included in the group to be disdained, as is the case with lust and greed). Through our adoration of these lesser idols, our worth is also compromised and we become less than what we set out to worship.

In order for our humanity not to be diminished—and to keep us from thinking of God as pet-owner, Gestapo, or neighbor—we've got to understand that God is our friend, and that our friend lives inside of us (Romans 8.11; 1 Corinthians 3.16).

Most of the time most of us forget this last part, that God the Holy Spirit lives in us, and so we try to make our spiritual way forward without the benefit of being God's friends.

We neglect the Spirit within us,
>because we cannot conceive of God being our friend;
>>so we try to achieve spiritual victory without God's help,
>>and we fail because the only way for us to succeed
>>>is through the Spirit.

That's why I think it's important to split hairs about "following Jesus." We don't follow Christ, *per se*. That road leads, again, to an overemphasis on our ability to copy. We have Christ in us. This road leads to a proper understanding that we are carriers, or hosts, of his Spirit, his Kingdom, and his mission.

> The incarnation is both once-and-for-all and ongoing, as the One who was and is to come now is and lives his resurrection life in and through us. Incarnation doesn't just apply to Jesus; it applies to every one of us...we have been given God's Spirit which makes Christ real in our lives. We have been made, as Peter puts it, partakers of the divine nature.
> **Len Sweet and Frank Viola**

The Incarnation is the foundation for our friendship, our participation, with God. He called us His friends. Friends share. We share in the life of Christ, just as we share in his suffering.

It's time we all understood just how embedded we are with God, so that we can live free from guilt over past sins, free from spiritual failure resulting from ignoring God, and free from loneliness and spiritual isolation.

> He is not our neighbor.
>> He is not our Policeman.
>> He is not our Owner.
> He is our friend.

>> And He is here to help.

QUESTIONS FOR FURTHER REFLECTION

1. What do you think of when you read the term "friend of God?" Is that a difficult image for you to accept? If so, is it because it feels too familiar – as if you're not giving God the respect He's due? Or, is it because it feels too awkward – as if you're not sure God is all that interested in having a buddy? Or, is it for another reason altogether?

2. Of the three un-friendly images used in this chapter, which do you resonate most with – God as neighbor, God as Gestapo, or God as pet-owner? Why?

3. How do you think understanding that your friend, God, lives in you and works in you to mature you spiritually is different than just "following Jesus?"

CONCLUSION

When I was a kid I used to love staying in hotels. In particular, I loved staying at the Double Tree Inn at SeaTac airport, something I got to do whenever my mom and I would accompany dad on his many business trips. We'd drive down the night before he'd fly out and the three of us would swim in the pool, eat at a restaurant, and I'd make a fort in the tub.

Sheer childhood ecstasy.

Our favorite game in the pool was for mom and dad to throw a dollar coin (we're from Canada, eh?) into the deep end and have me dive for it. I'd splash into the water like a side of beef and struggle down like I was having a seizure before finally emerging, red-eyed and vomiting chlorine, with the pearl of great price.

I think it's that feeling that compelled God to come down to earth.

I think He knew exactly what waited for Him at the bottom of the world and He struggled and fought and died to get it—to get us—and to bring us back above the water and keep us from sinking so low ever again.

He descends, and we all ascend together.

I want you to know how sweet you are to God. If a parent is only as happy as their least happy child, then please know and understand that God is agonizingly pursuing your pleasure and joy, fighting to bring you out of the depths of this life and into the beauty and goodness of His new life in you.

Peace.

dr. david mcdonald,
November 1, 2009

REFERENCE LIST

On the Incarnation, Saint Athanasius

The Humanity of God, Karl Barth

The Gospel of John, F. F. Bruce

Advent and Christmas, G. K. Chesterton

The First Christmas, Marcus Borg and John Dominic Crossan

Vintage Jesus, Mark Driscoll and Gerry Breshears

Visual Faith, William A. Dyrness

Envisioning the Word, Richard A. Jensen

The Word Made Flesh, Ross Langmead

Tome to Flavian, Leo the Great of Rome

Incarnation, Allister McGrath

A Community Called Atonement, Scot McKnight

Advent and Christmas, Thomas Merton

Advent and Christmas, Henri J. M. Nouwen

Thomas Aquinas, Theologian, Thomas F. O'Meara

Revisiting Relational Youth Ministry, Andrew Root

A Magna Carta for Restoring the Supremacy of Jesus Christ, Leonard Sweet and Frank Viola

LaVergne, TN USA
10 November 2010

204328LV00005B/3/P